if I were king

advice for President Trump

Edited by Harry Blazer and Elana Freeland

Introduction by Catherine Austin Fitts

ISBN-10: 1544242395

ISBN-13:978-1544242392

Cover art by Sharon Gay Snider   sharon@copplestoneworks.com

Table of Contents

The Premise

You have been elected King of the USA by a supermajority of the popular vote and have the support of the masses and a mandate for change. You have full authority to do whatever you want. There is no Congress. There is no Supreme Court. Whatever you declare becomes "the way." You cannot be assassinated. You can choose the amount of time you want to rule, and when you are ready to step down, you can put in place whatever form of government you think will best serve the nation going forward.

What would you do?

INTRODUCTION

The U.S. Presidential Election:
THE PRODUCTIVITY BACKLASH[1]

By Catherine Austin Fitts

"Because the part of America that grows your food, produces your energy and fights your wars believes the country needs a course correction." ~ Jim Barnacle, Harrisburg Pa, on why he voted for Trump

"There is a huge fight happening inside the United States right now between two factions. One faction wants to sacrifice the U.S. for the sake of the empire, and the second faction wants to sacrifice the empire for the sake of the United States." ~ The Saker, *"3rd Quarter Emerging Multipolar World,"* Solari Report By Catherine Austin Fitts

Last Saturday morning I enjoyed a long Irish breakfast in a hotel in Dublin reading global commentary about the U.S. presidential election. The discussion in both North America and Europe missed any appreciation of the economics at work, including three trends that we have covered in depth this year on the Solari Report:

- The shift to a multipolar world
- The end of the debt-financed growth model
- The importance of productivity growth

If the Trump election reflected a backlash, it was the backlash of the productive against the subsidized, particularly the *richly* subsidized.

THE GEOGRAPHY OF THE 2016 PRESIDENTIAL ELECTION: CENTRALIZATION VS. DECENTRALIZATION

If you look at a U.S. map that shows the results of the election, you will note that the areas that voted for Clinton represent the largest urban areas enjoying the highest benefits from the centralization of the economy through government spending, programs, heavy regulation, invasion of privacy and monetary and market interventions – much of it supporting a global empire. This includes Wall Street, Washington, DC, Hollywood and Silicon Valley.

The *New York Post* described it aptly in "Trump's voters were 'hidden' in plain sight":

> *Voters are rejecting big government, big banks, big corporations and big technology. They said no to establishment Republican primary candidates and Wall Street, and they hid from the political statheads trying to track their mood… Republican media strategist Bruce Haynes challenges his Republican and Democratic DC-based peers who are knee-deep in their drinks over Trump's win to take a step back and look at the map of what Clinton won Tuesday night. "She won the biggest metropolitan areas in the country and a couple of Southwestern states that have seen a huge influx of Mexican immigrants," he said. "And that is all she won and not a damn thing else." That is, she won the top 10 populations centers where most of the wealth, commerce and power is located — and lost*

the bulk of America... "Look, elites don't understand why America needs to be great again because for them America is great," said Haynes. Their economy is strong, their lifestyle is comfortable and the communities they live in, in and around New York and Washington, are the wealthiest and most influential in the country...[2]

THE MISES INSTITUTE DEMONSTRATED THIS DYNAMIC LOOK AT INCOMES

The Mises Institute noted that *"none of this matters for a media and investors who only pay attention to data in the form of huge national aggregates. After all, the national data shows the economy is growing. So everything must be fine. For millions of people outside the coastal cities where powerful investors and media figures live, however, things are not fine."*

If the Democratic Party had wanted to win the election, it would have nominated Bernie Sanders. However, the goal was not for the Democratic Party to win. The goal was for Wall Street, Washington, Hollywood and Silicon Valley to win. The "soft revolution" or "color revolution" was merely a front. This is one reason why so many people in the Republican establishment also supported Clinton.

A deputy assistant secretary in the Clinton administration once told me, *"Black people are hopeless. We are moving them out*

and moving the Hispanics in." The Democratic strategy in this election reflected that immigration strategy.

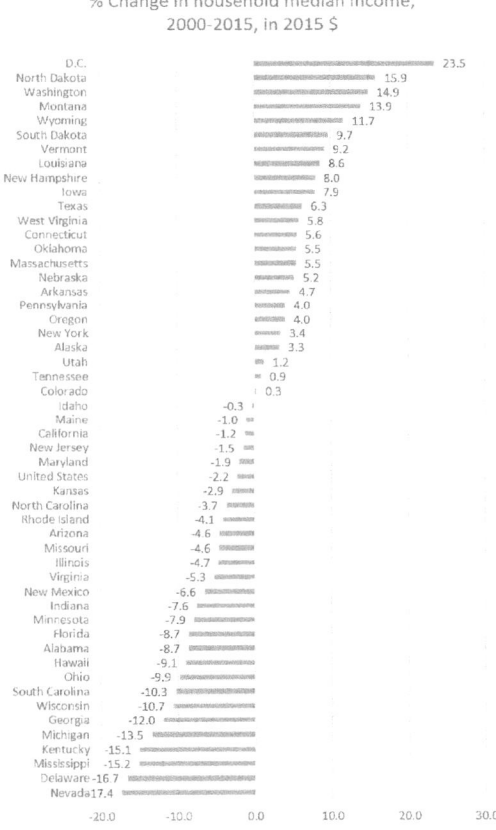

% Change in household median income,
2000-2015, in 2015 $

D.C.	23.5
North Dakota	15.9
Washington	14.9
Montana	13.9
Wyoming	11.7
South Dakota	9.7
Vermont	9.2
Louisiana	8.6
New Hampshire	8.0
Iowa	7.9
Texas	6.3
West Virginia	5.8
Connecticut	5.6
Oklahoma	5.5
Massachusetts	5.5
Nebraska	5.2
Arkansas	4.7
Pennsylvania	4.0
Oregon	4.0
New York	3.4
Alaska	3.3
Utah	1.2
Tennessee	0.9
Colorado	0.3
Idaho	-0.3
Maine	-1.0
California	-1.2
New Jersey	-1.5
Maryland	-1.9
United States	-2.2
Kansas	-2.9
North Carolina	-3.7
Rhode Island	-4.1
Arizona	-4.6
Missouri	-4.6
Illinois	-4.7
Virginia	-5.3
New Mexico	-6.6
Indiana	-7.6
Minnesota	-7.9
Florida	-8.7
Alabama	-8.7
Hawaii	-9.1
Ohio	-9.9
South Carolina	-10.3
Wisconsin	-10.7
Georgia	-12.0
Michigan	-13.5
Kentucky	-15.1
Mississippi	-15.2
Delaware	-16.7
Nevada	17.4

-20.0   -10.0   0.0   10.0   20.0   30.0

At 0:36 in the video "Map Shows Sanctuary City Islands of Blue in Sea of Red,"[3] overlays of the "sanctuary cities" with the blue dots in the red areas show a strategy by which the rich attempt to control the political machinery with engineered immigration targeted for strategic locations. As Ann Coulter pointed out, make 30 million immigrants legal and you are talking about the end of the system as we know it.[4]

This is also one of the reasons why the leadership of Wall Street, Washington DC, Hollywood and Silicon Valley has so vigorously opposed efforts to publish the U.S. budget and financial statements by Congressional district.[5] Doing so would only document the rich subsidy flowing centrally and the extent to which it is shrinking total national wealth.

THE SHIFT TO THE MULTIPOLAR WORLD

There are serious problems with leaving the current crew of richly subsidized in control. Their attempts to cover their overhead while engorging their coffers by extending centralization globally for a few more years are putting the entire world at risk. We have discussed this in the Solari Report this year in our series with The Saker, "The Emerging Multipolar World."[6]

Clinton's strength was on the financial side of the "central banking warfare model." This strength included the Neocons who promote a vision that the United States must maintain a global empire – the unipolar vision. The result has been exploding expenses for foreign wars, a military stretched globally, an explosion of dead and wounded and a European continent now being overrun by refugees from an imploding Middle East, as one civil infrastructure after another is destroyed. Along with this crime, we have fed the military-industrial complex a global arms industry and a mercenary capacity that has created an ever more powerful constituency for war.

This war-making edifice is expensive. It needs rich subsidy to keep it funded. Wars are funded with pubic dollars generating private profit. The public cost for each dollar of profit keeps rising. And it does not leave the U.S. military in good shape. One of the signature military affairs promoted by Hillary Clinton as Secretary of State was the invasion and destruction of Libya. Libya went from being the richest country in Africa to a country where one out of three people lives in poverty. We are all still trying to figure out where Libya's 143 tons of gold went, let alone how much is related to contributions to the Clinton Foundation and campaign.

In the *New York Times,* Tom Friedman wrote of the refugees pouring into Europe, "The lucky few find ways to get smuggled into Spain or Germany, via Libya. Libya was like a cork on Africa, and when the U.S. and NATO toppled the Libyan dictator — but did not put troops on the ground to help secure a new order — they essentially uncorked Africa, creating a massive funnel through chaotic Libya to the Mediterranean coast."

So we have trillions of dollars lost or missing in Middle East wars that explode American government debt, destroy numerous countries and overrun Europe with refugees. Yet it was expected that Clinton would give us more of the same, including war with Russia.

The Trump campaign represented many that must implement and fight wars both foreign and domestic – the generals, the intelligence agencies and the enforcement arm. It also included the states that send the most young people into the military and receive back the most caskets and wounded warriors.

A growing number of these professionals understand that the unipolar vision has reached its limits and that the United States must draw back behind the Atlantic and Pacific oceans and become more economically self-sufficient. This pullback is part of the rebalancing of our economic relationship with China[7] at the center of the shift to the multipolar world. This is part of the effort to create a new grand strategy.[8]

Call it "Fortress America," if you like. The move to repatriate corporate cash and offshore funds into North America, to continue to develop energy independence, and to rebuild our infrastructure and core military capability represents such an adjustment.

The military-intelligence side of the central banking warfare model wants to re-gather its energy. It does not want to engage in wars it might not win. Not to mention, with lead responsibilities to maintain the U.S. dollar as reserve currency and emerging developments in the South China Sea, the U.S. Navy has better things to do in a dangerous world than transgender training.[9]

THE END OF THE DEBT-FINANCED GROWTH MODEL

For decades, we have financed global growth with exploding levels of public and private debt. We covered this trend in our 1st Quarter 2015 Wrap Up: Planet Debt.[10]

The Clintons rose to personal wealth and power swimming upon a sea of expanding debt that funded the centralization of ownership and control, including the Neoliberal vision of maintaining and extending a unipolar world. When Bill and Hillary came to Washington, our official national debt stood at $4 trillion. After the financial *coup d'état* of trillions of dollars in bailouts and missing money, the official national debt now approaches $20 trillion. Underfunded retirement obligations and contingent liabilities will take it much higher.

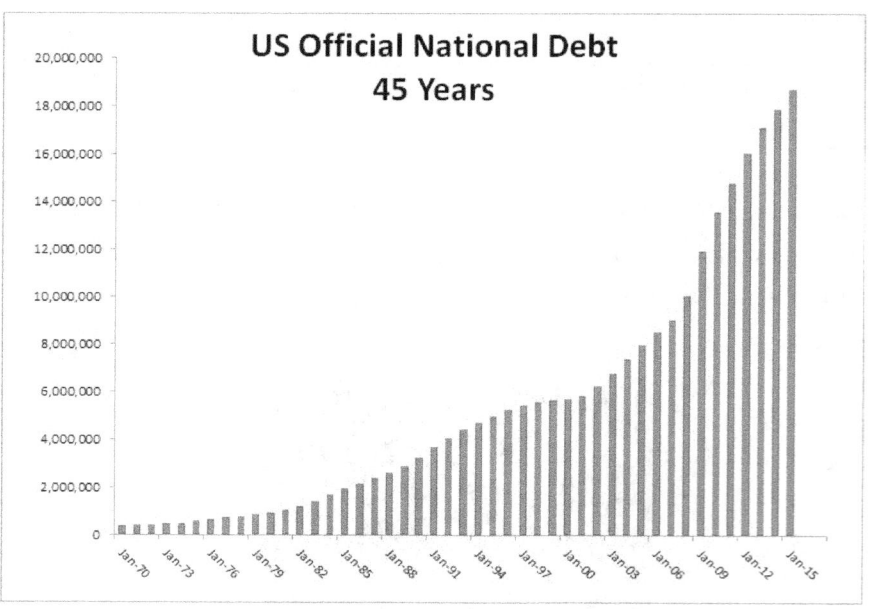

US Official National Debt
45 Years

Gary Christenson www.deviantinvestor.com February 2016.

The debt grew with globalization, which meant that the American middle class lost jobs and income. That did not have to happen. There were ways of addressing the needs of the middle class that could have resulted in a very different outcome. (See my online book *Dillon Read & Co. Inc. and the Aristocracy of Stock Profits*[11] and Sir James Goldsmith's Globalization Warning.[12]) That middle class loss of status and economic strength is clearly seen in the debt that American children incur to finance a college education.

Exploding levels of student debt have also correlated with a more expensive academic infrastructure, which has been used to support and justify the Neoliberal vision.

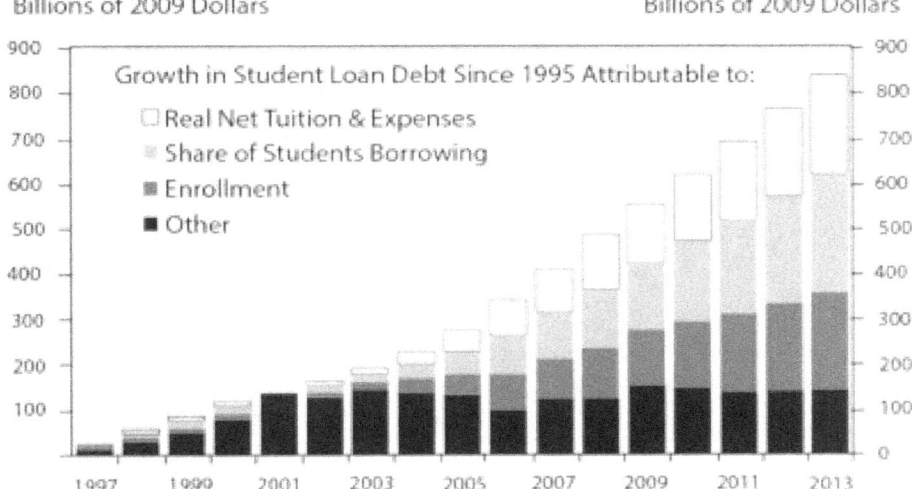

Billions of 2009 Dollars   Billions of 2009 Dollars

Growth in Student Loan Debt Since 1995 Attributable to:
☐ Real Net Tuition & Expenses
▨ Share of Students Borrowing
■ Enrollment
■ Other

Many of the adjustments to lending laws and student loan laws which allow predatory practices were made during the Clinton administration. See my piece on the Financial Hit Man of Student Loans.[13]

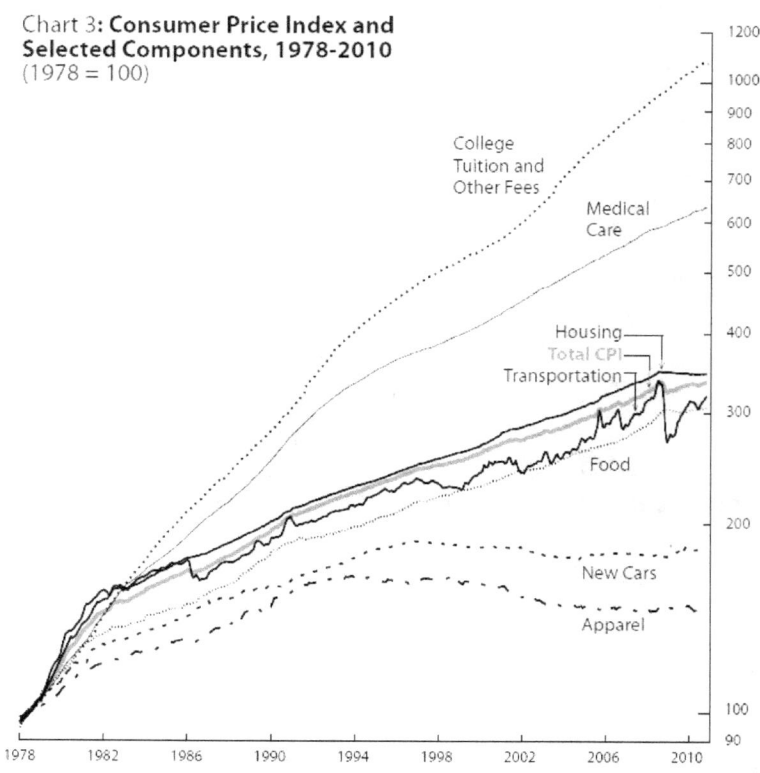

Chart 3: **Consumer Price Index and Selected Components, 1978-2010** (1978 = 100)

College Tuition and Other Fees

Medical Care

Housing
Total CPI
Transportation

Food

New Cars

Apparel

High-level student debt appears to be one of the reasons why the next generation of Americans is delaying homeownership. This is one of the reasons that the U.S. homeownership rate has fallen to its lowest levels since 1965.[14]

Exhibit 1: Causation or Coincidence?

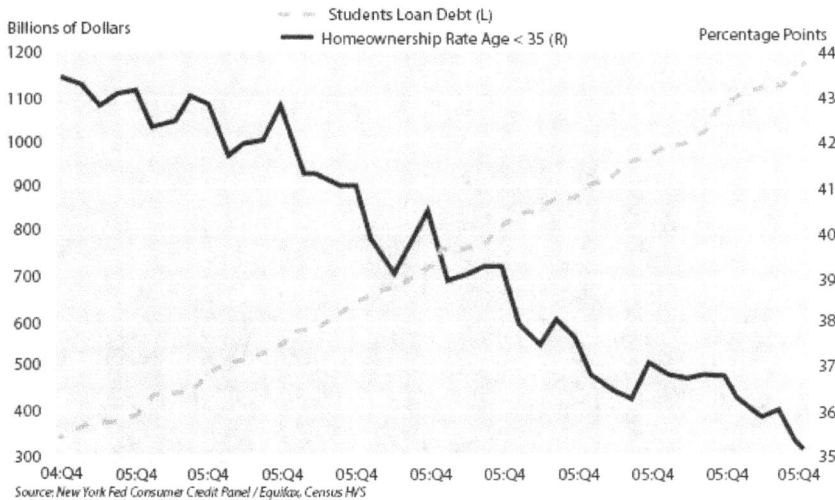

Source: New York Fed Consumer Credit Panel / Equifax, Census H/S

Another factor in the fall in homeownership rates is the devastation caused by the housing bubble first engineered by the Clinton administration. This bubble included massive foreclosures resulting from unaffordable levels of mortgage debt and a cost of trillions of dollars in taxpayer-funded bailouts.

Historical Foreclosure Activity

■ *US Properties with Foreclosure Filings*

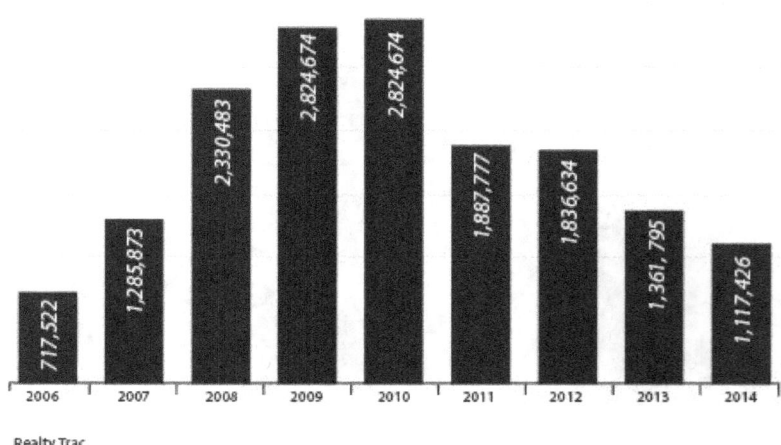

Year	Value
2006	717,522
2007	1,285,873
2008	2,330,483
2009	2,824,674
2010	2,824,674
2011	1,887,777
2012	1,836,634
2013	1,361,795
2014	1,117,426

Realty Trac

One of the ways in which sovereign governments have serviced increasing debt loads has been by engineering interest rates to record lows, particularly with the use of derivatives and significant central banking intervention. This drop in interest rates represents a significant transfer of wealth from savers and retirement accounts to governments and large borrowers – one of the reasons why pension fund and retirement underfunding will become one of the most pressing issues in both North America and Europe.

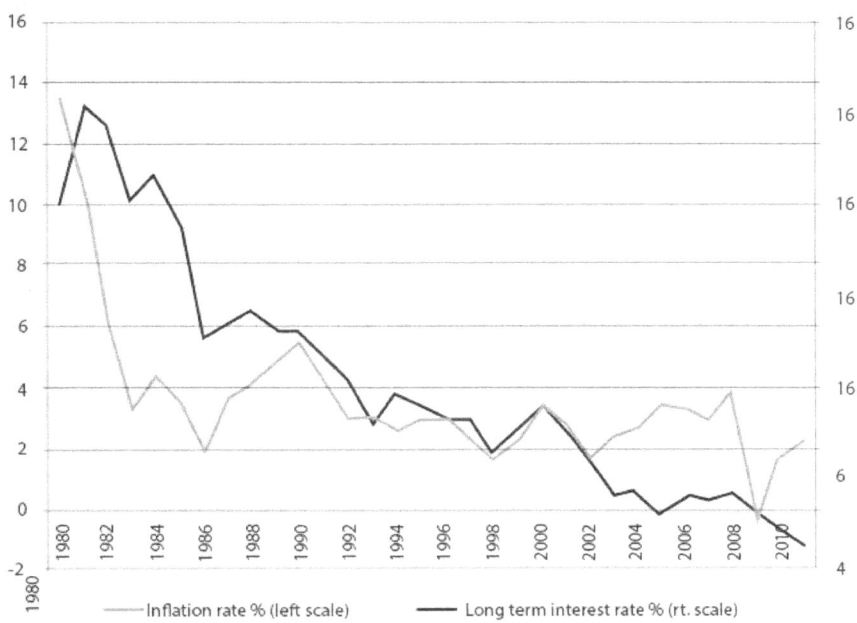

Inflation vs Long term rates

Inflation rate % (left scale)
Long term interest rate % (rt. scale)

I have written a great deal about this historical gush of government credit and spending. (See Financial Coup d'Etat,[15] The Myth of the Rule of Law,[16] Coming Clean Beyond the Fiscal Cliff.[17]) This coverage shows what is now over $50 trillion in bailouts and "undocumentable adjustments" missing from the U.S. government. The U.S. Department of Defense reported $6.5 trillion in undocumentable adjustments in fiscal 2015 alone – approximately $20,000 for every person in America. See my commentary: "Criminal vs. Crazy Man: Cut and Run, Monica Lewinsky II, & Real Trouble Ahead."[18]

This extraordinary commitment of resources has funded extraordinary and uneconomic centralization in a manner which has harmed the general economy, the environment and productivity – a significant expenditure of government money that has had a "negative return on investment." This is why I believe that the #1 fiscal priority of every American should be to bring transparency to the federal budget, including where the missing money has gone and how we can get it or the related assets back.

Such discovery must begin with transparency for the federal budget and financial statements for our individual Congressional District.[19]

Our ability to finance with debt has depended on the willingness of the world to hold U.S. dollars and U.S. treasury securities and corporate debt. In part, the push to extend the unipolar vision is a push to ensure that governments around the world continue to do so. The shift to a multipolar vision means that our capacity to print infinite amounts of paper in exchange for valuable natural resources has reached its limits.

This is why all year I continue to quote the German finance minister Wolfgang Schäuble who stated at the G20 meeting in Shanghai: "The debt-financed growth model has reached its limits… There are no shortcuts that aren't reforms."[20]

The debt party is over. If anything, the Trump victory represented the people in the military and intelligence community who know better than to try to extend it with more war. The shift to the multipolar world is upon us. A growing number of people responsible for managing the central banking warfare model want to draw resources back to North America and rebuild the center.

This means that the negotiations over the U.S. federal budget are going to be significant in the first year of a new administration. The budget is where most of the real policy changes will play out.

A FEW MORE CRITICAL STATISTICS: PRIVATE PRISONS AND LIFE EXPECTANCY

What the Deputy Assistant Secretary of HUD in the Clinton administration told me in 1994 about black people bears more thought. Black people were indeed "moved out" with predatory lending – they lost their homes – and with incarceration as the Clinton administration support for the war on drugs, expanded prison sentences and contracts to private prisons exploded. I have described the growth of the private prison complex during the Clinton administration in my online book *Dillon Read & Co. Inc. and the Aristocracy of Stock Profits.*[21] The result was the growth of a significant prison industrial complex in the United States. The U.S. now boasts the highest incarceration rate in the world.

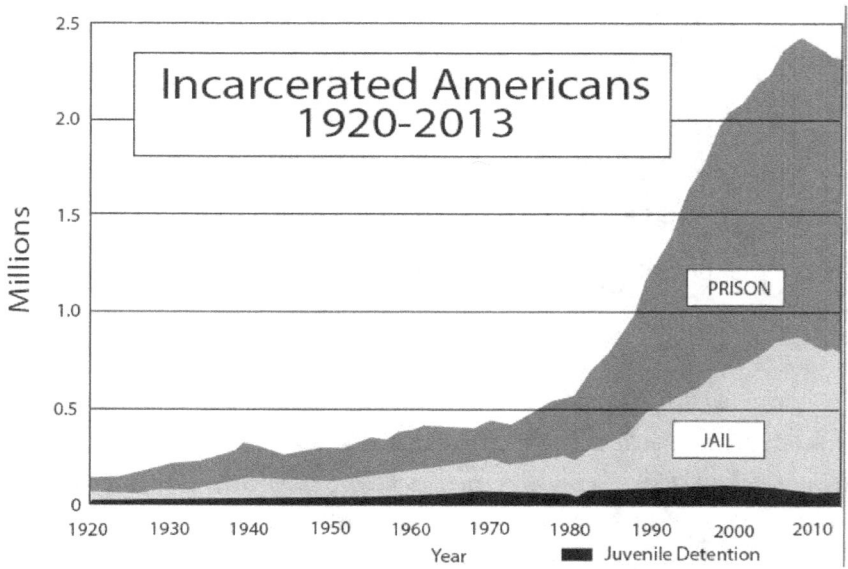

Incarcerated Americans 1920-2013

PRISON

JAIL

Juvenile Detention

International Rates of Incarceration per 100,000

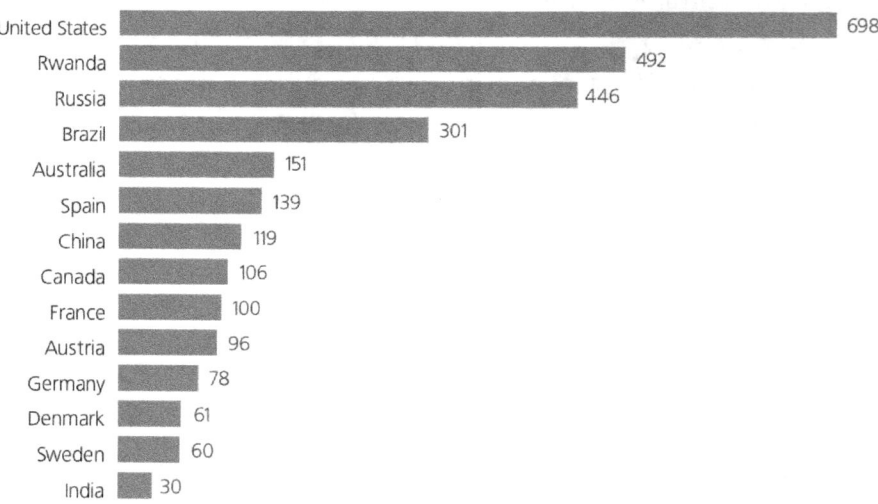

United States	698
Rwanda	492
Russia	446
Brazil	301
Australia	151
Spain	139
China	119
Canada	106
France	100
Austria	96
Germany	78
Denmark	61
Sweden	60
India	30

Source: Walmsley, R. (2015). *World Prison Brief*. London: Institute for Criminal Policy Research. Available online: http://www.prison-studies.org/world-prison-brief

18

One reason why the Clintons were successful in building this machinery is due to the largesse they showered on minority elites to help them accomplish it. This success is one of the reasons we are hearing screams about "whitelash."[22] The last thing that folks who helped round up and gentrify their poorer brethren for a profit want to do is look in the mirror. (See my commentary, "Trump & the African-American Elite Gravy Train: The Party's Over."[23])

While poor minorities were rounded up into prisons, poorer Caucasians were not faring well either. They were also losing their homes in record numbers as predatory loans and foreclosures swept through their communities, businesses and farms. In fact, the life expectancy of white women without a high school diploma, dropped by 5 years between 1990 and 2008. By 2008, life expectancy for black women without a high school diploma had surpassed that of white women of the same education level.[24] (The same study showed that life expectancy of white men without a high school diploma dropped by three years.)

If you review life expectancy statistics in the United States, Hillary Clinton tended to carry the areas with the higher life expectancy whereas Donald Trump carried the areas with lower life expectancy. Another way to explain these facts is that the people whose life force was being drained while government was engineering rich subsidies to Wall Street, Washington, Hollywood and Silicon Valley, were looking for a way to stop that drain. They were, in fact, trying to stay alive.

THE IMPORTANCE OF PRODUCTIVITY GROWTH

This brings us to the importance of productivity growth discussed in depth in our 2ⁿᵈ Quarter Wrap Up: Productivity, Prosperity & the Popsicle Index.[25]

Meeting retirement goals and other financial obligations requires continued productivity growth. The problem is that productivity is not growing. In my discussion of productivity in the 2nd Quarter Wrap Up, I divided productivity between labor productivity (workplace) and human productivity (outside the workplace). In summary, my thesis is that recent increases in labor productivity have been achieved at great cost to human productivity. Moreover, the benefits of increased labor productivity are not shared. While labor productivity has grown steadily, hourly compensation has flatlined.

GROWTH OF REAL HOURLY COMPENSATION FOR PRODUCTION AND NONSUPERVISORY WORKERS VERSUS PRODUCTIVITY (1948 – 2011)

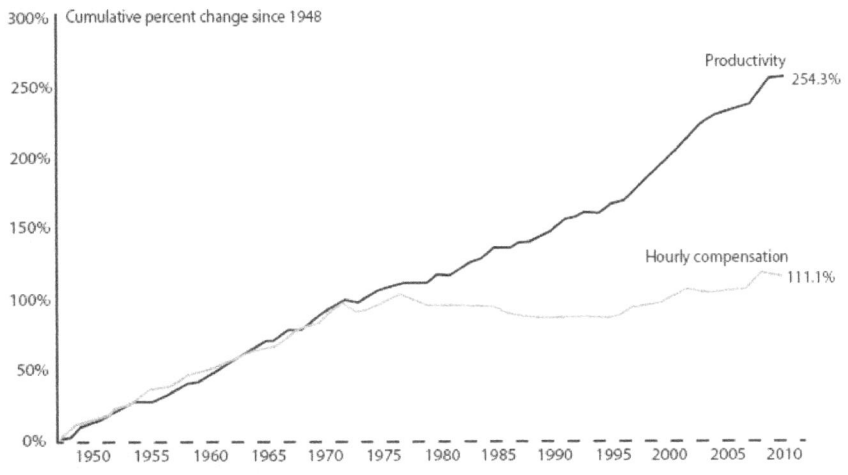

One of the hopes for increased productivity is the reengineering of government, education and health care – three areas that have maintained high levels of employment while private corporations were downsizing. This generally means that (i) the tax burden to Americans has been heavy as their incomes flatlined, and (ii) the return on their savings fell as expenses steadily inflated. I often refer to this steady squeeze of the average person and family as the *slow burn*.

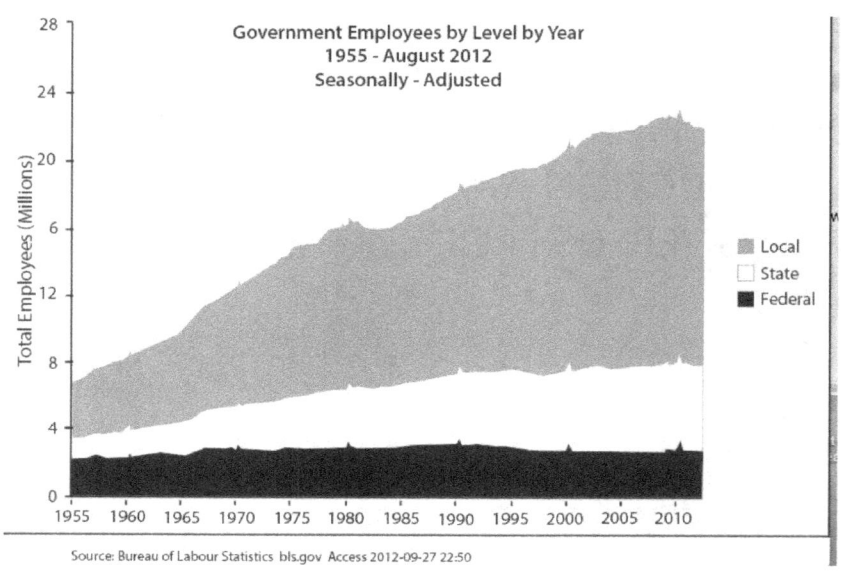

Government Employees by Level by Year
1955 - August 2012
Seasonally - Adjusted

Source: Bureau of Labour Statistics bls.gov Access 2012-09-27 22:50

Although there is potential to reengineer government, education and health care (as described in the 2nd Quarter Wrap Up), the approach by the Obama Administration was seriously flawed. Obamacare, policies regarding health care records, and Common Core were among the leading policy reasons for the Democratic defeat in the 2016 elections — and with very good reason. We need to get these changes right to generate productivity for Americans, not simply generate more invasive intelligence and profits for Silicon Valley. Let Silicon Valley be held to the standard of creating increased labor and human productivity as opposed to engineering surveillance capitalism that turns Americans into prey.

LEADERSHIP

If you live and work in the heartland of America as I do, you spend a lot more time among people who are required to run family budgets, small businesses and farms. They tend to do more concrete functions such as plumbing, construction, trucking, farming and manufacturing. They've spent a lifetime mastering the art of covering their costs. They understand that you have to "sell something for more than it costs you to make it." They are not central bankers or presidents and cannot create money out of thin air. Their financial world is accountable. Even state and local governments are required to balance budgets.

A former CIA officer schooled in covert operations once told me that my problem was that I did not appreciate that the average IQ in America was 103. My response is that a person with an IQ of 103 who has spent a lifetime balancing budgets and scrambling to generate income in a world that only writes a check for real value-added, will be able to cope much better in a world without debt growth than a person with an IQ of 150 who graduated from Harvard or Yale and has been floating on richly subsidized operations in large urban centers ever since.

The first person understands that "you have to sell it for more than it costs you to make it." The second person is floating in a mystical bubble of inflated prices that depend on debt growth to finance activities that promote and justify central control – activities that do not add fundamental value to the economy.

Another thing that first person understands is that one of the keys to productivity is that men and women must give each other energy.[26] Divide-and-conquer politics are hugely destructive to labor and human productivity. Another issue is meritocracy – "may the best man win." Affirmative action is too expensive and too complex. It is fascism with a progressive façade. And an exploding number of rules and regulations are destroying productivity across America.

Increasing U.S. productivity is essential and the people who understand how to increase productivity growth are pushing back. They want leadership that can lead us back to fundamental productivity growth. We can no longer afford people who are good at manufacturing more rules, blowing debt bubbles and engineering financial fraud. The long-term bull in the bond market is over.

HILLARY CLINTON HAS A NEGATIVE RETURN ON INVESTMENT TO THE AMERICAN TAXPAYER

Hillary Clinton lost the 2016 election. While I believe that there were significant shenanigans and vote rigging on both sides of the aisle, I believe Clinton lost the popular vote and the electoral vote (despite any news reports to the contrary). Let's look at some of the reasons why Hillary Clinton has been getting steadily richer while many of the productive people in America have been getting steadily poorer.

It is worth comparing Clinton's profits on speeches at Goldman Sachs (who benefited richly on the end of Glass-Steagall[27] during the Clinton administration and bailouts during Obama/Clinton, among many other policies) to what professionals in American earn. While millions of people were losing their homes and funding bailouts, Hillary Clinton was buying and living in multimillion-dollar mansions in Washington and New York.

After Libya, one of the worst examples of Clinton-style disaster capitalism was Haiti, which we discussed with Dr. Dady Chery in our Solari Report, Haiti & Disaster Capitalism.[28] Following the Haiti earthquake in January 2010, Bill Clinton as Special UN Ambassador and Hillary Clinton as Secretary of State literally took control of Haiti. The Clinton Foundation raised enormous sums of money that never reached the Haitian people. To this day, the many questions about where the money went continue to go unanswered.

Chelsea Clinton was married six months after the U.S. invasion of Haiti. There are now allegations that Clinton Foundation funds helped pay for her wedding, which is estimated to have cost $3-5 million. One wedding website described Chelsea's wedding cake as follows:

We talked to Chelsea's cake baker from La Tulipe Desserts for a few of the details. The nine-tiered cake was 500 pounds and four feet tall, and price estimates fall in the $10,000 to $12,000 range. The cake was mostly white with silver accents and 1,000 edible white sugar flowers, all delicately brushed to give a pearlescent sheen. The gluten-free (Chelsea's allergic to gluten) vanilla wedding cake with dark chocolate mousse filling was made out of local and mostly organic ingredients.

Imagine how many Haitians would be alive today if the Clintons had allowed $3 million more of the money they raised for the Haitians to actually go to the Haitian people. Imagine why someone planning on running for President would spend $10,000 or more on a wedding cake while the Haitian people were dying for lack of shelter and safe drinking water or innocent Americans were working in private prisons as slave labor to make uniforms for the military. Of course, we all know what happened to the woman who said, "Let them eat cake."

Americans are a remarkably generous people. They have no problem with wealthy people who earn money through hard work, innovation or good luck. They do have a problem with politicians and political appointees who make money by selling influence and using the taxpayer credit to engineer private benefits – including for themselves – that shrink the pie. The average American knows that, in the long run, you have to make money by baking pies instead of stealing other people's pies.

As allegations poured out from Wikileaks regarding the Clinton campaign and the Clinton Foundation, Americans got a taste of how "pay to play" really works, how manipulation of classified information is used to create private fortunes and even how treason possibly occurred.

Hillary Clinton is part of a syndicate that has grown in wealth and power by centralizing control in the U.S. in a manner that has drained the productive people who create much of the economic wealth that financed it. There were many people who voted for Trump in the 2016 election who voted for Obama in 2008. The productive wanted change eight years ago. What they got was a transfer of $27 trillion in bailouts – more than all the retirement savings in the country – to the large banks and private interests.

With debt-financed growth coming to an end, the productive were not prepared to tolerate the continued drain.

Clinton was shrinking the pie of productive people who do not want to be liquidated to keep the empire going. This was not about race, sex or any of the divide-and-conquer, politically correct waste-of-time air cover used to stalk the general population in support of empire building. Clinton lost because of a productivity backlash.

CONCLUSION

So what happens now? Will President Trump be able to lead the U.S. towards lasting change?

Rejecting Clinton and the Neocons is the first step. Now inaugurated, President Trump and Vice President Pence have assumed leadership of a complex machinery that is deeply dependent on harvesting global and domestic subsidy. Turning that machine around is easier said than done. Yes, the productive people want change. However, that change requires a broad-based commitment to shift the fundamental dependency of the U.S. establishment and general population away from the central banking warfare model. The richly subsidized, in particular, are in no hurry to convert to becoming fundamentally productive. Do we see Hillary Clinton embracing the opportunity to learn how to drive her own car or to clean her multiple homes? In my experience, there is no one meaner than the richly privileged when they are suddenly required to earn their keep.

Here is what Col. Lawrence Wilkerson, former chief of staff at the State Department under General Colin Powell, said regarding the challenge before all of us:

> The two candidates that we have just had offered to us in this election, both of them made comments and one of them had a profession that dictated this … that they were going to continue to play by that playbook. Now one wonders what one of them is going to do because he [Trump] is bouncing all over the place. Is he going to rewrite the playbook? Is he going to play by the playbook? Is he going to throw it out the door? What's going to happen?
>
> That uncertainty certainly unnerved the markets initially, they recovered today. And they will continue to recover as long as he remains somewhat conciliatory and doesn't look like he is going to throw the playbook out. Just imagine if he suddenly decided that he would and it might be beneficial to the country that he did.
>
> Then you see what I am talking about now because the markets will go all over the place again. Because the markets are part of this state. The markets are part of waging war. They are part of the warfare state. Our entire financial system now is geared to this warfare state. It has an umbilical cord extending from it. That's how it survives. That's how it makes a lot of its profits … directly or indirectly.

Not for nothing was HSBC found out for laundering drugs. You know where a lot of those drugs were coming from? … Afghanistan. This is a vicious many-headed animal that we have allowed to grow up – as Eisenhower predicted – and if we are not careful it is going to eat all of our lunches before it is through with us.[29]

The task before the new administration is much greater than most people appreciate. Since the election, millions of dollars have flowed to engineer protests, and vindictive corporate media are doing their best to sabotage the transition. The political establishment is trying to build political tollbooths at every turn. This change will not be decided by an election. This is trench warfare, involving all of us.

What can we do? Peggy Noonan addressed it in her column in the *Wall Street Journal,* "What Comes After the Uprising" (November 11, 2016). She closed with some exceptionally sound advice:

"The next president needs you.

This is our country.

HELP HIM."

Give thanks that Hillary Clinton is not President of the United States. As Winston Churchill once said, "Nothing in life is so exhilarating as to be shot at without result." We have missed a very big bullet – one that could have destroyed America. Now we go to work, each in our own way. If the productive want a country where we are once again free to be productive, if we want America to be great again, it is going to take all of us pulling in that direction every day for the next four years.

Notes

1. This essay, replete with graphs, can be found in its entirety, with hyperlinks, at https://solari.com/blog/the-us-presidential-election-the-productivity-backlash/.

2. Salena Zito, "Trump's voters were 'hidden' in plain sight." *New York Post*, November 9, 2016. http://nypost.com/2016/11/09/trumps-voters-were-hidden-in-plain-sight/

3. The Alex Jones Channel, "Map Shows Sanctuary City Islands of Blue in Sea of Red," November 10, 2016, https://www.infowars.com/map-shows-sanctuary-city-islands-of-blue-in-sea-of-red/.

4. "WND TV: Ann Coulter: If Hillary wins, she will amnesty 30+ million illegal aliens," *WorldNetDaily*, http://www.wnd.com/wnd_video/ann-coulter-if-hillary-wins-she-will-amnesty-30-million-illegal-aliens/#iGbwFlVi1imRq73g.99.

5. Catherine Austin Fitts, "Open Letter to My Congressman." *The Solari Report*, March 16, 2016, https://solari.com/blog/open-letter-to-my-congresswoman/.

6. See *The Solari Report*: "Russia and Global Geopolitics with the Saker," February 3, 2016; "The Saker: A Unipolar vs. Multipolar World," April 2, 2016; "The Emerging Multipolar World with Saker: Russia, Ukraine & the Risks of War," June 7, 2016; and "The Emerging Multipolar World with Saker: Russia, Syria & Recommendations for a Trump Presidency," September 30, 2016.

7. Catherine Austin Fitts, "Special Report: Stephen Roach – Seeking US/China Balance." *The Solari Report,* June 18, 2014.

8. Catherine Austin Fitts, "Book Review: The New Grand Strategy." *The Solari Report,* August 12, 2016.

9. Hope Hodge Seck, "Navy to Hold All-Hands Training, Webinars on New Transgender Policy." *Military.com,* September 16, 2016, http://www.military.com/daily-news/2016/09/16/navy-to-hold-all-hands-training-webinars-new-transgender-policy.html.

10. Catherine Austin Fitts, "Solari Report 1st Quarter Wrap Up: Planet Debt." *The Solari Report,* April 22, 2015.

11. http://www.dunwalke.com.

12. "Sir James Goldsmith's 1994 Globalization Warning," *The Solari Report,* February 1, 2010: The Charlie Rose interview with Goldsmith, "A prophetic interview with Sir James Goldsmith in 1994 Pt1," uploaded in 2010 by vantagepointmoon.

13. Catherine Austin Fitts, "William M. Diefenderfer: The Financial Hit Man of Student Loans." *The Solari Report,* September 23, 2011.

14. Catherine Austin Fitts, "Meditations on the Falling US Homeownership Rate." *The Solari Report,* August 8, 2016.

15. Catherine Austin Fitts, "Financial Coup d'Etat." *The Solari Report,* August 8, 2011.

16. Catherine Austin Fitts, "The Myth of the Rule of Law, or How the Money Works: The Destruction of Hamilton Securities Group." *2001 Third Quarter Commentary*, http://solari.com/assets/PDFs/myth_of_the_rule_of_law.pdf.

17. Catherine Austin Fitts, "Coming Clean Beyond the Fiscal Cliff." *Solari Special Report*, http://solari.com/articles/beyond_the_fiscal_cliff.

18. Catherine Austin Fitts, "Crazy Man Versus Criminal: Cut and Run, Monica Lewinsky II, & Real Trouble Ahead." *The Solari Report*, October 1, 2016.

19. Catherine Austin Fitts, "Open Letter to My Congressman," March 16, 2016; republished at *The Solari Report* on February 14, 2017 with this CAF comment: "In light of the political changes underway, I am republishing this letter I wrote last Spring to my Congresswoman. If you have time to pay attention to news from DC, you have time to send a copy to your Congressman. Real solutions are going to happen county by county in 3100 counties. Congress is gridlocked because real solutions are not going to happen centrally."

20. "German finance minister: expansive policies may have laid foundation of next crisis." *Reuters*, February 25, 2016, http://www.reuters.com/article/us-g20-china-schaeuble-idUSKCN0VZ0BG.

21. http://www.dunwalke.com.

22. Josiah Ryan, "'This was a whitelash': Van Jones' take on the election results." *CNN*, November 9, 2016,

http://www.cnn.com/2016/11/09/politics/van-jones-results-disappointment-cnntv/.

23. Catherine Austin Fitts, "Trump & the African-American Elite Gravy Train: The Party's Over." *The Solari Report*, March 3, 2016.

24. Sabrina Tavernise, "Life Spans Shrink for Least-Educated Whites in the U.S." *New York Times*, September 21, 2012, http://www.nytimes.com/2012/09/21/us/life-expectancy-for-less-educated-whites-in-us-is-shrinking.html.

25. Catherine Austin Fitts, "2nd Quarter Wrap Up: Productivity, Prosperity & the Popsicle Index." *The Solari Report*, July 7, 2016.

26. Catherine Austin Fitts, "Promoting Women Part I." *The Solari Report*, March 30, 2014.

27. The Glass-Steagall Act (the Banking Act of 1933, 48 Stat. 162), passed by Congress in 1933, prohibited commercial banks from engaging in the investment business. Nearly 5,000 banks failed during the Great Depression.

28. Catherine Austin Fitts, "Haiti & Disaster Capitalism with Dr. Dady Chery." *The Solari Report*, July 1, 2016.

29. Transcribed by Catherine Austin Fitts from the video "State Of US Empire: Former Bush Aid Lawrence Wilkerson, Mnar Muhawesh, Rev. Antal Panel," published November 12, 2016 by MintPressNews: "For Armistice Day, the Minneapolis torture committee headed by FBI whistleblower Coleen Rowley hosted a discussion at First Unitarian Church to discuss the state of the US corporate Empire. Panelists include former Bush aid and

chief of staff Colonel Lawrence Wilkerson, Reverend Chris Antal (former army chaplain in Afghanistan), and MintPress editor Mnar A. Muhawesh."

- *Visual graphs and information provided by www.solari.com, all information has been vetted.*

- *Special thanks to the Government Agencies*

- *Walmsley,R (2015) World Prison Brief, London: Institute for Criminal Policy Research.*

- *Realty Trac.*

- *Gary Christenson www.deviantinvestor.com February 2016*
  http://deviantinvestor.com/about-me/

It's so good to be King

Jon Rappoport

Good evening, my fellow Americans. I'm coming to you through my brand new Royal Network, which brings you the truth 24 hours a day, every day.

Tonight, in my first talk, I'm going to touch on many issues—skipping along from one to another. Stay alert. Follow the bouncing ball.

My ascension to the throne is recent, so I want to acquaint you with where I stand.

And sit.

As I recline in my bejeweled throne for the very first time (it fits beautifully!), I breathe a sigh of relief. Finally, I'll have a chance to enact my dreams and make them fact in the world.

Do I want to build an orbiting city in the clouds? Do I want a mountain of gold? Do I want to deploy my unlimited police powers? Do I want to build an enemies list and embark on a stirring program of revenge? Will blood flow in the streets?

Power. The contemplation of it is engaging, to say the least, since I can actually use it, since I can override all objections with the stroke of a pen. Mine is a long crow feather. Listen to the royal scratchy sound as I set my name on the parchment with a flourish.

But here is a thing to consider: *the power to make individuals more powerful.* To make them more free.

Such people would be the company I desire, the company I want to keep. And the rule of non-interference is easy enough to understand. Be as free as you want, so long as you don't interfere with another's freedom. A child can comprehend it.

All right. Buckle up. Here's chapter one of my long and winding laundry list—

I want urban farms in every city in America. Plots of land where local residents grow and trade and eat their own fresh, clean, nutritious food. It is a revolutionary act. I want 10,000 of these farms in inner cities. My government will provide initial funding in the form of loans. The residents themselves will expand their operations into profit-making ventures; they'll sell their excess food.

I'm estimating that for less than $100 million, the whole program can be launched—as opposed to the trillions of dollars that have been poured down rat holes for the past 50 years in the "war on poverty."

The residents of inner cities will now have a real stake in their own survival and success, and they will escalate the power of their demands for safe neighborhoods—safe from gangs and thugs and drugs.

I think it's time George Soros and David Rockefeller stand trial for their crimes against the people. So be it. (That was a quick thought and I didn't want to forget it.)

All federal agencies must submit their proposed regulations to be voted on as bills.

That may seem like a small and inconsequential thing, but I assure you it's not. Wake up. For decades, these rogue criminal agencies have been essentially making laws on their own and it will now stop. They can no longer pretend they're framing new rules in accordance with established law, when in fact they're twisting meanings for their own nefarious ends. Attorney Jonathan Emord has pointed this out many times. He is absolutely correct. For his wisdom, I should award him a state— Virginia, perhaps. But I'll hold myself back for the moment on that score.

Hmm. Rather than donate Virginia to Emord, I have another idea. Make it a state in which the following unimpeachable law applies: any health practitioner of any stripe can practice freely, as long as he does not offer remedies which are more toxic than the standard medical remedies for the condition he is treating. Do you see the outcome? Virginia, overnight, becomes a destination of choice for huge numbers of people who highly value freedom. The economy of Virginia blossoms like a million roses. Virginia becomes an example for every other state in the union. They quickly follow suit.

(Yes, there is still a union of states, even though I am King. I want the states to flourish. I want them to take back the powers granted them by the Constitution. I want the federal government to shrink drastically. And so it will, by my hand.)

Another quick hitter: also by my hand, a hundred completely honest attorneys (the search for them may take a bit of time) will be elevated to the rank of prosecutors and will undertake The Case Against Bill and Hillary Clinton and the Clinton Foundation with the same vigor of hunters pursuing man-eating tigers that have been decimating their villages.

Jefferson envisioned public education as a training ground for citizens of the Republic, a form of government that had never been attempted on such a broad scale before. Education will return to this endeavor. Pronto. Courses in logic, the Constitution, individual freedom, individual power—commencing from the earliest grades possible. The entirety of Common Core will be dumped into a giant fire pit and burned to a crisp. New generations of entrepreneurs and visionaries will be birthed.

The FDA, the CDC, and NIH (National Institutes of Health) shall immediately be disbanded, and their employees, where necessary, investigated and prosecuted for crimes. Since at a minimum, the U.S. medical system kills 225,000 people a year, or 2.25 million people per decade (Starfield, 7/26/2000, *Journal of the American Medical Association*), the prosecutions will be rigorous and the sentences harsh.

Immediately, no person shall be forced to take a vaccine under any conditions. Or to put it another way, NO PERSON SHALL BE FORCED TO TAKE A VACCINE UNDER ANY CONDITIONS.

I will appoint Dr. Peter Breggin to issue his already-completed reports on the profession of psychiatry. He will show, beyond the shadow of a doubt, that no so-called mental disorders have a basis in physical diagnostic tests and that the drugs for these so-called mental disorders are all toxic.

Psychiatrists will be barred from testifying in court cases and barred from all schools. Mental screening programs will stop at once. Lobotomy and electroshock (ECT) are hereby banned as torture. A multi-front case for scientific fraud shall be launched against the American Psychiatric Association.

The Department of Justice and the FBI will be reorganized from the ground up. Many employees will be fired. Two new divisions will be created: Sharks Against Corporate Crimes, and Sharks Against

Gangs. Their generous funding will be derived from vastly excess monies paid to big banks in the 2008 bailout. Those excess monies will be returned.

On the immediate list to be pursued: Pfizer, Glaxo, Monsanto, Dow, DuPont, Lilly. Just for starters. The basic case: poisoning the American people. Then come the big banks: deep fraud.

Wars of Empire will cease. A case against Barack Obama and Hillary Clinton will be pursued re the invasion and decimation of Libya.

I need to take a breath and regroup…

Good. I'm back.

Through me, Edward Snowden, Julian Assange, and Bill Binney (in charge) will issue detailed reports on the Surveillance State and the new and necessary scaling back of Big Brother. My edicts will follow.

NAFTA, CAFTA, GATT, the WTO, TiSA, and all other Globalist trade treaties are canceled. Jobs will be brought back to America. Through a combination of tax breaks, tariffs, and Royal pressure, corporations that have fled the U.S. and set up shop in the Third World will return. My DOJ Sharks will investigate them for crimes committed abroad: abuse of employees, violation of basic environmental regulations, etc.

How could I forget this one? The CIA is hereby disbanded. A third division in the DOJ must be formed: Sharks Against Government Agencies. We'll get the real history of the CIA. Prosecutions to follow.

Do you get the general drift here? There are many more items I will add to my list. Egregious government debt—no more. The end of the Federal Reserve. The curtailment of foreign aid. The elimination of other federal agencies—the Department of Education immediately comes to mind. The expulsion of the United Nations from America and the pursuant fumigation of its New York headquarters—an ideal location for more urban farms.

Immigration—yes, that thorny issue. By some estimates (and depending on how the count is done), the U.S. already has the greatest number of immigrants per capita of any nation in the world. Officials admit there is no procedure in place to vet the current flood of immigrants in order to root out terrorists. This is a dangerous situation. The flood must be curtailed. And what about immigrants taking jobs from Americans already living at the poverty level? And what about many people coming to America who have no intention of embracing basic values enshrined in the Constitution, but instead pursue whatever free services they can obtain? This whole situation must be remedied. I will demand an accurate accounting of the cost to the nation of the current immigration flood. I will act to curtail the flood.

Beyond these measures, I shall take up a role as an educator. With wide-open channels of communication available to me via my Royal Network, I will embark on a series of talks to the American people. These talks will cover a wide range of subjects. This will be my personal school, a school always in session.

Here are a series of quotes from talks I have already composed:

"What does it mean to be an American in this new epoch? What journey are we undertaking? Is it one in which every person submerges his or her own dreams in favor of the needs of the group? Is that what we are after, a collective spirit that drowns all other concerns? Is that what you want? Constant pressure to give in and surrender your lives to the Whole?"

"I see you deciding to be free and independent. I see that vision, and I am warmed by it. I see that power rising. I see people throwing off chains of dependence on the government. Who claims that is wrong? On what basis are they claiming it? What is their agenda? I will tell you this: they are pursuing a dead end. I cannot abide a nation of helpless victims. Nor do I think you can, either."

"What do you say, America? Should human beings become stronger and more self-reliant? Or should they become weaker? What is the goal? I hear you saying stronger, don't I? Isn't that obvious? Is there some inherent virtue in weakness you and I are missing? If we are aiming at a renaissance, and we are, doesn't that mean stronger is better than weaker? Who's kidding whom here? Correct me if I'm wrong, but can't schools teach strength and self-reliance? Of course, they can."

"Are you afraid of people who own guns and don't shoot anyone? Or are you more concerned about people who have guns and shoot people? Wouldn't you like to know who is committing the bulk of gun crimes in America? I would. I'm waiting for a report on my desk in three hours, and I'll have an answer for you. Then I'll order a plan, a real plan, not a fake one, for arresting, prosecuting, and sentencing the people who are illegally firing bullets at others. And I won't back down."

"Taxes? I may be a little headstrong here, but my best thought at the moment is: abolish the federal income tax. The federal government will have to get along on a sales tax on goods and services. Five percent. If we can't sell enough in this country to support the federal establishment, the establishment will have to shrink. Give me a little more time to think this through. At any rate, I want to get rid of the IRS."

Those are a few excerpts from my fireside chats.

Next: understand the difference between pinpoint attacks on known terrorists and wars of opportunity. Afghanistan is a good example. What did we achieve there, aside from the remarkable expansion of opium-poppy growth?

If other nations want to defend themselves, let them, but we are not the policemen for the world. Our primary military mission is self-defense here at home. Period. This is why I'm ordering most of our overseas troops to come back.

Here is an excerpt from a talk to the American people I'll be delivering from my fireside soon. It was researched by my staff of "wild dogs," as I like to call them. "Let the hounds loose!" I offer it as an illustration of how major media lie and deceive, which I will offset as King by putting the full force of my new far-reaching Royal Network in the service of keeping Americans informed. Wouldn't you like the truth with your dinner?

Don't accept the slogans about American medicine. "It's the best in the world." "People are being denied treatment." "We must take care of our citizens."

How about this far more accurate slogan: "Let's force more Americans to die in the care of doctors."

The American healthcare system, like clockwork, causes a mind-boggling number of deaths every year.

On July 26, 2000, the U.S. medical community received a titanic shock when Dr. Barbara Starfield, one of its most respected public-health experts, revealed her findings on healthcare in America. Starfield was associated with the Johns Hopkins School of Public Health. The Starfield study, "Is US health really the best in the world?" published in the *Journal of the American Medical Association*, came to the following conclusions:

Every year in the US there are:

* 12,000 deaths from unnecessary surgeries;

* 7,000 deaths from medication errors in hospitals;

* 20,000 deaths from other errors in hospitals;

* 80,000 deaths from infections acquired in hospitals;

* 106,000 deaths from FDA-approved correctly prescribed medicines.

The total of medically caused deaths in the U.S. every year is 225,000. That's 2.25 MILLION deaths per decade, which makes the medical system the third leading cause of death in the U.S. behind heart disease and cancer.

The Starfield study is the most disturbing revelation about modern healthcare in America ever published in the mainstream.

Next: Wherever you see organized psychiatry operating, you see it trying to expand its domain and its dominance. The Hippocratic Oath to do no harm? Are you kidding?

The first question to ask is: Do these mental disorders have any scientific basis? There are now roughly 300 of them. They multiply like fruit flies.

An open secret has been bleeding out into public consciousness.

THERE ARE NO DEFINITIVE LABORATORY TESTS FOR ANY SO-CALLED MENTAL DISORDER.

And along with that:

ALL SO-CALLED MENTAL DISORDERS ARE CONCOCTED, NAMED, LABELED, DESCRIBED AND CATEGORIZED by a committee of psychiatrists from menus of human behaviors.

Their findings are published in periodically updated editions of the psychiatric bible known as *The Diagnostic and Statistical Manual of Mental Disorders (DSM)*, printed by the American Psychiatric Association.

For years, even psychiatrists have been blowing the whistle on this hazy, crazy process of "research."

Of course, pharmaceutical companies that manufacture the highly toxic drugs to treat these "disorders" are leading the charge to invent more and more mental-health categories so

they can sell more drugs and make more money.

In the PBS Frontline episode "*Does ADHD Exist?*" Dr. Russell Barkley, an eminent professor of psychiatry and neurology at the University of Massachusetts Medical Center, unintentionally spelled out the fraud:

> PBS FRONTLINE INTERVIEWER: Skeptics say that there's no biological marker—that [ADHD] is the one condition out there where there is no blood test, and that no one knows what causes it.

> BARKLEY: That's tremendously naïve, and it shows a great deal of illiteracy about science and about the mental health professions. *A disorder doesn't have to have a blood test to be valid. If that were the case, all mental disorders would be invalid... There is no lab test for any mental disorder right now in our science.* That doesn't make them invalid.

Oh, indeed, that does make them invalid. Utterly and completely. All 297 mental disorders. They're all hoaxes. Because there are no defining tests of any kind to back up the diagnosis.

You can sway and tap dance and bloviate all you like, and you won't escape the noose around your neck. We are looking at a science that isn't a science. That's called fraud. Rank fraud.

There's more: Under the radar, one of the great psychiatric stars who has been out in front inventing mental disorders went public. He blew the whistle on himself and his colleagues. And for years, almost no one noticed.

His name is Dr. Allen Frances, and he made VERY interesting statements to Gary Greenberg, author of the *Wired* article, *"Inside the Battle to Define Mental Illness"* (December 27, 2010).

Major media never picked up on the interview in any serious way so it never became a scandal.

Dr. Allen Frances is the man who, in 1994, headed up the project to write the latest *DSM-IV* to define and label and describe every official mental disorder, all 297 of them. In the April 19, 1994 *New York Times* piece, *"Scientist At Work,"* Daniel Goleman called Frances "perhaps the most powerful psychiatrist in America at the moment…"

Well, sure. If you're sculpting the entire canon of diagnosable mental disorders for your colleagues, insurers, the government, and Pharma selling the drugs to match the 297 DSM-IV diagnoses, you're right up there in the pantheon.

Long after the DSM-IV had been put into print, Dr. Frances talked to *Wired*'s Greenberg and said the following:

"There is no definition of a mental disorder. It's bullshit. I mean, you just can't define it."

BANG.

If I Were King
(Advice for Donald Trump)

The Saker

(written purposefully in editorial style)

Introduction

The surprise election of Donald Trump offers the United States a wide range of amazing opportunities for change on all levels, from the way the USA runs its economy to a radical change in U.S. foreign policy. It should be noted, however, that this is not the first time that a new U.S. President enters office with enormous political capital that could, potentially, be invested in real, meaningful change.

It would not be an exaggeration to say that following the tragic events of 9/11, the entire planet was united in sympathy and support for the USA. Even countries that are nowadays presented as archenemies, such as Russia and Iran, immediately and sincerely sided with the USA and offered their help. Then, following eight years of stupidity, arrogance, incompetence and imperial hubris, the people of the USA voted in Barak Obama with his promise of real change and "Yes we can!" The Nobel Committee went so far as to grant him a Nobel Peace Prize just for not being Dubya and for making promises that Obama, of course, never kept. In 2009, there were real hopes that finally the horror would end, but again, another eight years of stupidity, arrogance, incompetence and imperial hubris followed.

Then the people of the USA voted in Donald Trump with yet another promise of real change and "making American great again." Trump might end up being a Dubya v2 or "Obama reloaded," but there is also the real possibility that he might not. Two things strongly suggest that he might bring *real* change to the USA:

1) The U.S.-run Anglo Zionist Empire is in a deep crisis and simply cannot continue to double-down after each failure (the "program," so to speak, of Hillary Clinton). The Empire is crashing and something must be done to save whatever can be saved.

2) There are real signs that the U.S. ruling elites are turning on each other and have roughly split into two groups: one led by Clinton, who wants to sacrifice the USA for the sake of the Empire; and one led by Trump, who wants to sacrifice the Empire in order to save the USA.

If my assessment is correct, the following is the single most important geostrategic factor facing the new U.S. President: the Anglo-Zionist Empire is collapsing and the only two options are (1) a controlled process, during which the USA will be able to obtain the best terms possible for this planetary draw-down, and (2) the collapse is catastrophic and possibly cataclysmic.

As a nation, the USA simply cannot afford another Dubya or another Obama, both of whom offered only denial of reality and ideological mantras. What the USA needs is a pragmatist President who will try to get the best deal he can for his country. How? The USA is still an immensely powerful nation, and while the Empire is most definitely coming down, nobody out there, no nation, would benefit from a cataclysmic collapse of the USA. Major nations, including Russia and China, would much prefer a controlled transformation of the USA from a planetary hegemon to a "normal" (if powerful) country to a conflict with the USA, even if at the end of the day the USA would lose.

There is another reality that must always be kept in mind: it makes no sense to change a person and not change the system. The only real, meaningful change comes from a change of the system itself, from a regime change and not just an administration change. Trump has been elected President, which means that the top several thousand officials of the Executive Branch will be changed, but this does not necessarily mean that the system itself will change. And since the system, the polity, is clearly imperial in nature, purpose, function, organization, and ideology, this system will resist any attempts at modification, never mind replacement. On January 20, 2017, the struggle for change began and has already proven to be a brutal and ruthless struggle. Think of it as a war for survival between the United States and the Anglo-Zionist Empire. Only one side will walk away while the other will be defeated and eliminated.

So how should Donald Trump wage this war for the survival of the United States?

INTERNAL U.S. POLITICS

During his Presidential campaign, Trump indicated on numerous occasions that the U.S. corporate media was totally unfair to him, that it was being used as a strong propaganda tool for the Clinton campaign, and that most journalists were dishonest when it came to their coverage of him. This did not change in January.

No matter what Trump does, the few groups who own the vast

majority of the U.S. media continue to use their power and influence to discredit, ridicule and misrepresent everything that Trump does. Simply put, the U.S. propaganda machine is attempting to sabotage any and all efforts of the Trump administration.

The solution is obvious: Trump needs to create his own TV channel, modeled after *RT (Russia Today)*, and use it to communicate directly with the American people. Like Vladimir Putin's *Direct Line* call-in show and Hugo Chávez's *Suddenly With Chavez*, he should organize call-in shows so regular people can ask him questions and he can use such calls to explain what he is trying to achieve. It makes no sense whatsoever to hope that mainstream media will suddenly become fair, or that by appeasing those who run the U.S. media, he will get a better chance. Not only does Trump have the money to launch his own TV channel, he could even make it profitable. "Trump TV" could combine news with less than politically correct reporting, free debates and discussions, talk shows and interviews with those who never get to speak on "official" U.S. TV channels. Most importantly, Trump needs to create his own "information conglomerate" that combines Trump TV with Internet-based social media in order to directly and frontally attack the corporate media for being just a propaganda tool in the hands of a small cabal. At the same time, Trump should lobby Congress to pass legislation to break up the current media conglomerates and encourage alternative and independent media, especially on the Internet (Net neutrality).

Next, Trump must strike the Congressmen, special interests, lobbying firms, public relations groups, think tanks, etc. forming the backbone of the hegemon control over the U.S. polity. The method of attack is as obvious as it is effective: get them for corruption, obstruction of justice, mismanagement, dereliction of duty, incompetence, conspiracy to defraud, and all the other possible crimes that they have been committing for at least 16 years now. Before Trump, the globalist elites were so sure of their impunity that none of them could resist the temptation to get a little chunk of the pie. The advantage of this method of "draining the swamp" is that it is absolutely legal. Even better, it will merit huge support from the American people who fully realize that the system is corrupt to the bone. All Trump needs to do is to get the right person to run the FBI and create a special task force for corrupt public officials.

Considering how fantastically corrupt the Pentagon is, it will be simple to rapidly purge it of the worst elements, along with the various members of the U.S. intelligence community. Trump could also do what Putin did with the oligarchs in Russia: offer that they will be left alone in exchange for their support. A "be good and I will let you be, or else..." kind of offer they won't reject. Once Trump's key enemies get busy fighting for their own personal survival, it will be much easier to force them to accept structural changes in the U.S. polity. Also, offering a way out for those who will not resist instead of seeking retribution should minimize the number of people who will have nothing to lose. The goal must remain draining the swamp, not retribution.

The role of PR will be crucial. Trump should directly address the American public, appeal to support from the "American street," and explain what he is doing at every step. Trump alone, even with powerful backers, probably does not have the authority or power to completely purge the cabal from power, but if he does it while claiming the mandate and support of the people in the name of democracy, then he might be able to sufficiently weaken the cabal until they fold and surrender like the oligarchs did in Russia.

Trump supporters will have to be mobilized by simple, straightforward slogans and goals like "We are taking American back" or "Fight for me and I will fight for you" or "Make America American again." The simplicity of crude slogans will be crucial to mobilize as many people as possible. The best example is how Recep Tayyip Erdoğan convinced the Turkish street to stand up and defend him against the 2016 coup d'état attempt. Of course, it is unlikely (but not impossible) that the cabal will attempt a coup against Trump. But well-presented, the simple claim that Trump "needs help" or "is in danger" will mobilize those who are truly fed up with the current system. Patriotism has always been used in the USA to rally the people, and in this case it could even be used for a legitimate and decent purpose: to liberate the USA from the "new world order" Empire and its minions.

There are, of course, also those who are currently completely freaking out because they were exposed to the rabid anti-Trump propaganda in the U.S. media. These are the folks who are contemplating moving to Canada, who attend cry-ins on college campuses, who demonstrate with "Not my President" signs and are in need of therapy to overcome the horror of Trump being elected instead of Clinton. These are not folks who could be rationally convinced, but there might be some steps that would immediately make Trump more popular even with them. For example, on the "internal front" Trump could:

- Legalize marijuana on a federal level
- Abolish both the DEA and the ATF
- Abolish the Patriot Act and restore pre-9/11 civil rights
- Abolish all federal laws restricting the 2nd Amendment

These four measures would not only make the USA a much better country to live in, but they would also send a strong message that the Trump administration is strong on civil rights and liberties.

On the economic front, Trump should announce the end of crony-capitalism à la Obama and a return to true free market economics "for the people" and not "for the bankers." To that end, he should

- Abolish the privately owned Federal Reserve and have the U.S. Treasury take over its functions
- Nationalize all the banks that Obama bailed out in 2008
- Demand that Congress re-regulate Wall Street and the U.S. banking system

Finally, Trump should not just abolish Obamacare but replace it with a viable singer-payer system as has been done in every single developed country on the planet. American exceptionalism should not mean that the American people are treated exceptionally badly, which is all that it means today. Various models make it possible for private insurance companies to compete for contracts, but all of them place the ultimate burden of supporting the seriously ill not upon a for-profit entity but upon society as a whole. Not to do so in the 21st century is simply uncivilized.

Last but not least, on the internal front Trump should begin to re-shape the public discourse that has been hijacked by various minorities and special interest groups. To do so, he should repeat over and over again that the real purpose of democracy is not to protect minorities against the majority but to protect the majority against the minorities, lest the latter become the only ones to enjoy the protections and benefits of the political system. The proclamation of such a radical crimethink – "democracy is here to protect the majority against the minorities" – will, of course, result in a phenomenal backlash from said minorities, but it will also, and for the first time, mobilize millions of disenfranchised Americans who have been left completely abandoned and even exploited by the system. The power of the minorities backlash can be used by Trump to prove his case that democracy in the USA is threatened and that special interest groups (a politically correct euphemism for "minorities") are trying to take control of the country against the will of the vast majority of the American people.

ON FOREIGN POLICY

Foreign policy can offer Trump something which U.S. internal politics cannot: immediate and tangible results. The biggest blessing for Trump is that all of the major crises the USA is facing on the external front are completely artificial creations of the Obama Administration, and that the USA has the means to rapidly defuse them.

The number one foreign policy goal for Donald Trump should be to make Russia into a global international partner. Not necessarily a friend or ally but a trustworthy partner with whom the USA can work. The way to do that would be to immediately convene a week long (or more) conference with Vladimir Putin. Besides Donald Trump and Vladimir Putin, all the U.S. and Russian senior national security officials and their staffs should attend, as well. The straightforward agenda should be to solve all the outstanding issues between the USA and Russia, including:

- The war in Syria
- The civil war in the Ukraine

- European security issues

The good news is that solutions to all three of these crises are really self-evident.

In Syria, the USA should abandon the notion of overthrowing President Bashar al-Assad and focus on destroying all the terrorist groups currently operating in Syria, including those whom Obama considered "good terrorists." Once this is achieved, the USA and Russia could offer the Syrian government a roadmap for the decentralization and democratization of Syria, realizing that at the end of the day, Syria's reformation should be decided by the Syrian people themselves, not by Russia or the USA. It is enough that the two superpowers offer their recommendation and expertise, which Syrians will have a hard time ignoring. The single most important political goal of the U.S. and Russia in Syria must be to recognize Syria as a sovereign and independent country for whom no outside actors – Russia, the USA, Turkey, Saudi Arabia, Israel, Iran, etc. – can impose their plan. Furthermore, no outside actor can occupy any part of Syria under any pretext, nor force the partition of the country. This way of thinking is neither earth shattering nor radically new nor outlandish; it is simply recognition that international law also applies to Syria. Restoring international law to Syria will solve the Syrian conflict.

The same approach should be taken by Russia and the USA concerning the Ukraine. International law and norms include the right of Ukrainians to have self-determination. However, before that right can be exercised, law and order need to be restored. The means to do this have already been agreed upon by the UN Security Council: the Minsk Agreements. These Agreements must either be implemented by all parties, including the Nazi regime in Kiev – the Neo-Nazi party Svoboda – or declared dead, in which case Russia and the USA need to act jointly to recognize the de-facto break-up of the country into at least two entities and convene a peace conference to secure the future peaceful coexistence of these two entities. What is obvious is that the U.S. support for the Neo-Nazi regime was an immense mistake and the consequences have been terrible for the Ukraine.

The USA and EU bear a direct responsibility for what has happened and they must now not only work with Russia to restore peace and security to the Ukrainian people but also agree to financially assist in the reconstruction of the Ukraine. Russia alone simply does not have the means to rebuild the Ukraine. (Note: For that reason alone, the notion that Russia would want to invade the Ukraine is absolutely ridiculous. Russia, with her rather small and struggling economy, cannot afford to take over even part of the Ukraine and in fact never intended to.)

Sooner or later, the USA, the EU and Russia will have to get together to prevent the Ukraine from turning into a giant black hole like Kosovo. The Ukraine is too big to be rescued or rebuilt by a single nation or alliance. Furthermore, the security situation in the Ukraine is so bad that it will require an international effort to restore peace and security, probably by means of a UNSC-sanctioned peacekeeping, peace-enforcement and police operation. A major long-term international effort by all the major parties in this conflict will be required to rebuild the Ukraine, whether as a unitary state or group of successor states. In order to make such an international effort possible, the Ukraine will have to be declared (in the Ukrainian Constitution) a neutral and non-aligned state that will not join any military alliance or host any foreign military forces.

The Ukrainian civil war also has to be considered in the greater context of European security. Here again, the solution is obvious: a return to the *status quo ante* before the deployment of NATO troops and the U.S. anti-missile system in Eastern Europe. These forces and systems must be withdrawn. In exchange, Russia must agree to withdraw her Iskander missile systems from her western borders. Following these initial steps, a new European treaty on conventional forces in Europe, similar to the Cold War era CFE Treaty, must be negotiated and signed between Russia and NATO member states. The ratification of such an agreement could usher in further agreements on tactical nuclear weapons, short and intermediate range ballistic and cruise missiles.

The bottom line is that Europe must be as demilitarized as possible, which falls nicely in line with Donald Trump's promise to make the Europeans pay for their fair share of NATO. Ideally, of course, NATO should be dismantled as a useless Cold War fossil and replaced by a new continental security organization including all the countries between the Atlantic and the Ural mountains. At the very least, NATO should be pulled back, de-fanged, and forced to accept the rather evident notion that security can only be collective, and if one party feels threatened, this compromises the security of all the parties. As for the European nations, they should unite their efforts towards the real dangers threatening Europe.

The crises in Syria and the Ukraine, plus the issue of the future of European security, can be dealt with in a relatively short time. At the very least, a number of basic roadmaps to solve these crises can be rapidly agreed upon. All that is required for that is to ditch failed ideological dogmas and a solid dose of common sense. By working together on jointly solving these crises, Russia and the USA would show the world that a new era of collaboration has begun, and that far from being enemies, Russia and the United States have decided to become partners. This U.S.-Russian partnership would finally make it possible for the international community to deal with two other, much more complex, crises:

- International (state-sponsored) terrorism
- The illegal occupation of Palestine by Israel

Unlike the Syrian, Ukrainian, and European security crises, these two crises won't be solved rapidly and will require a long-term sustained effort.

The ugly secret of terrorism (which everyone involved knows about) is that 95%+ of terrorism is state-sponsored. (There are exceptions, but they are rare and mostly unsuccessful.) Terrorism requires money, personnel, weapons, training, communications, etc., all of which is currently provided only by states.

The other ugly secret is that the United States and U.S. allies have been using Takfiri terrorists for decades as foot soldiers to destabilize and overthrow regimes they did not like. (I use this term loosely to include all instances and franchises of what is usually called "al-Qaeda," without going into the subtle distinctions between al-Nusra, ISIS, and the rest of them). From Chechnya to Bosnia to Kosovo to Iraq, Libya, and Syria – Takfiri terrorism is really one single phenomenon whose roots come from the war in Afghanistan. Other nations – including the Kingdom of Saudi Arabia (KSA), Turkey, Israel, and Qatar – have now adopted this model, but originally the phenomenon was born in the demented mind of Zbigniew Brzezinski and his CIA colleagues. The United States has to take the fundamental decision to stop using terrorist organizations and classifying them as "good" or "bad." In truth, the monster produced by the U.S. Deep State has now at least partially turned against the U.S. and the American people, and the priority now should be to deal with this monster.

Terrorist organizations can only be dealt with on two simultaneous levels: (1) people at the counter-terrorism level involving all the security branches of the state (state security, military, economic, public relations, communications), and (2) the ideas and values of terrorism at a spiritual-ideological level. On the first level, Russian and the U.S. agencies must cooperate, beginning with sharing all the information they have about terrorist groups. Then, Russia and the USA need to unequivocally tell all nations currently supporting terrorist organizations, whether covertly or overtly, that they must cease such support, and if they refuse to comply with this demand, there will be political, economic and possibly military consequences. The various terrorists groups need to be found, infiltrated, monitored, and destroyed. It is really that simple: just a matter of will.

On the second, spiritual-ideological, level, Donald Trump needs to understand that the USA cannot declare a war on Islam and hope to win. In the dialog between Russia and the USA, Russia needs to represent the Muslim world and convince the USA that nations like Iran, Syria or Iraq should be treated as valued and crucial allies and not lumped together with Saudi Arabia, Qatar and Turkey, the real sponsors of Takfiri terrorism. Furthermore, the USA needs to understand that only traditional Islam can defeat the Takfiri ideology (as opposed to the Takfiris themselves). In other words, the Russians need to convince the Americans to stop using Takfiris and stop waging war on Islam. This will be very, very hard, but there is no other option. If the

Americans insist on their war on Islam, they need to be told in no equivocal terms that if they persist on this self-defeating course, they will be on their own and will be defeated.

There will be no peace in the Middle East until the illegal occupation of Palestine by Israel ends. I personally believe that the Two State solution is dead and that the only real solution to this conflict is the so-called One State solution in which Israel abandons its racist ideology and accepts the basic principle of one-man, one-vote for all its citizens. Still, considering the monumental incompetence and corruption of almost the entire Palestinian leadership, Israel does not currently face enough pressure to even begin to consider a One State solution. The Palestinians have done pretty much everything wrong in the past two decades and there will be a price to pay for their blindness. So the solution, however bad and unpalatable, appears to be Israel in the 1967 borders plus a few exchanges of real estate here and there, backed by joint U.S.-Russian security guarantees for Israel *and* all of Israel's neighbors, including Syria and Iran. The message here would be simple: "You want peace – we will give it to you; if you don't – stop pretending like you do." Having the Russians in Syria is the best thing that could have happened both for Syria and Israel, and this opportunity should not be ignored.

However desirable they may be, none of the measures above really address the most important role Donald Trump could play in history: dismantling the Anglo-Zionist Empire and transforming the United State from an "imperial homeland" into a "regular country."

DISMANTLING THE EMPIRE

Any honest assessment of the current state of affairs in Europe, the Middle East or Asia will have to accept as self-evident and undeniable that the Anglo-Zionist Empire is collapsing, both internally and externally. The election of Trump is, in fact, the best proof of this internal collapse. The failure of the Obama administration to achieve anything, anything at all, on the foreign policy front proves that the USA has been essentially rendered powerless.

This can go down in one of two ways now: either the U.S. doubles-down over and over again, Neocon style, and risks a catastrophic collapse, or the U.S. can negotiate a draw-down and achieve an orderly retreat from its role as a wannabe world hegemon. What is needed is a strong and powerful decision to indicate that the USA is serious about this.

Donald Trump should therefore set up a commission of military and security experts and tell them to draft a new National Security and Military Defense Doctrine for the USA with the following goals to work toward:

1. At least 50% global reduction of the so-called "defense" budget (Green Party Candidate Jill Stein made this proposal);
2. A gradual withdrawal from and dismantling of all U.S. overseas military bases not deemed essential under the new military doctrine;
3. Restructuring of all branches of the U.S. Armed Forces into a much smaller but better trained and equipped force capable of dealing with the *real* threats to the United States and its allies;
4. A complete overhaul of the U.S. Intelligence Community,

beginning with the abolition of the CIA and merging the current sixteen intelligence agency into four agencies: a civilian agency, a military agency, a communications agency, and a presidential agency supervising and centralizing them all. This process would require Congress to pass a new Law on Intelligence which would provide a comprehensive legal definition and basis for U.S. intelligence operations;

5. Last but not least, the new U.S. National Security and Military Defense Doctrine will recognize that security is always collective, that as long as I am in fear, you are not safe. Security can only be achieved by *reassuring* the other side, not by threatening it. This idea should be the cornerstone of all these reforms.

The obvious policy goal here would be to replace power projection and hegemony enforcement with defense of the United States and U.S. allies. Eventually, NATO will therefore have to be dismantled and replaced by a European common security treaty.

Since the U.S. war machine, which spends more on "defense" than the rest of the planet combined, is also a crucial job provider for the American people, it will be necessary to offer all U.S. service men and women social guarantees for at least a 5-year transition period in which salaries, health benefits, pensions, etc. will be maintained and gradually phased out. The point here is not to punish those who serve in the military but to wean American society from its dependence on wars for economic stimulation.

One of the biggest positive side-effects of the adoption of a new National Security and Military Defense Doctrine will be that it will liberate immense sums of money to pay for all the other reform programs of President Trump, especially if it is combined with a merciless crackdown by the FBI on corruption in the Department of Defense and U.S. military-industrial complex. This will also make the U.S. Armed Forces much stronger, simply because corruption is one of the main causes for their current inabilities.

CONCLUSION

Donald Trump has become President at a time when the United States is facing the worst crisis in its history, and he has inherited a system fantastically evil and corrupt to the bone. Imperialism, violence, war, poverty and exploitation are all hard-wired into the modern American polity. It would take a miracle for one man to prevail against such odds. But miracles do happen, as we saw with Vladimir Putin in Russia. Will Trump become the "U.S. Putin"? I don't think this is likely, but I do believe it is possible. Expectations are a bad thing, both in life and in politics. But hope is a good mindset, as long as it does not turn into delusion. Who said that a billionaire couldn't love his country? As Ernesto "Che" Guevara wrote: "The true revolutionary is guided by a great feeling of love. It is impossible to think of a genuine revolutionary lacking this quality." I hope that President Trump will find enough love in his heart to overthrow the Empire and save the United States.

TYRANNOSAURUS RUMP

Sofia Smallstorm

Now I lay me down to sleep
I pray that Trump is not a creep
The country's ills are his to fix
I pray that he will play no tricks
If we should last another year
I pray his path is wide and clear
Let him be guided through the night
To wake us strong and safe and bright
    — Children's bedtime prayer

    The Electors did not defect from their pledges or show themselves to be faithless after all as wicked Democrats tried hard to thwart the Trump presidency. On December 19th, 2016 the Art-of-the-Dealmaker was awarded his crown and a green light to make America great again, as he had continually assured overflowing crowds who attended his rallies. It's all going to be beautiful, he told them over and over. And on January 20th, the creation of that beauty would begin.

    If Donald Trump were a dinosaur, he would be Tyrannosaurus Rump, standing tall and powerful on thunderous mega-legs with a burly torso and a crop of straw-orange hair. His little hands would be itching feverishly to fiddle with the mess we were in, to yank the plug on the muddy swamp and let it all gurgle out. His jaws would be swinging wide, all set to bite at the heads of the liars and cheaters and murderers who had corrupted and contaminated America's offices; the roar of his voice ready to blast the names of the new and deserving—friends and helpers who would not look to gain from their appointments in unmentionable ways. His tail—the Tyranno-tail—laced with heavy vertebral struts dwarfing those of his massive spine, would be felt by millions as it thumped the earth with his every decision, causing a shudder that shook the houses and rattled doors and blinds and even caused skyscrapers to sway. For this, he was called T-Rump. The name was the very sound of the dino-slap.

T-Rump was a frightening apparition in a business suit, with a jacket that constantly flapped around his copious middle, his mini-arms helpless to keep it under control. Across the country, as he strode onstage to deliver his speeches, people shrank at the sight of the hinged jaws embedded with a forest of dagger-like teeth. His heart was in the right place, they knew, despite the relentless attacks of the press who were doing all they could to keep a powerful reptile out of the highest office. And it was this, his heart, that kept them loyal.

For over a year they had chanted his name: "Tee-rump, T-RUMP!" whenever he was near. They waved pennants and wore caps embroidered with his Tyranno-shape; college bands had even marched across campuses playing a Tyranno-anthem—ta-rump, ta-rump, tarump-tarump-tarump. Now he was theirs, the fair-and-square winner of the toughest political race (no matter what the Democrats still thought), and his fine heart and roaring voice would repair their broken country just as he had pulled himself out of financial quicksands in his own complicated and challenging affairs. He was a reptilian survivor, and there were few who knew the ropes like he did. Of this the people were confident.

With the ugly Electoral hurdle behind them, the people had been sending him letters with their hopes and dreams outlined for him to read. His Transitional Team collected these letters, passing him the most interesting ones, which he kept in a folder by his bed. He reviewed them at night, sometimes three or four times each if they were very good. He would shake his big head in delight at certain ones, envisioning the future all lit up in dazzling sugar plums, just as he had when he had told the people, It's all going to be beautiful.

One of the letter writers advised him that nothing could be done to fix America unless he, T-rump, fired himself as Chief Executive Officer of the USA corporation. He summoned his Transitional Team to discuss this. "Of course, we must think of the country as a corporation," they reasoned. "It's the only way we're going to make it run right. But you can't fire yourself or we'll have no one to take directions from."

T-rump thumped his tail on the floor. "No, this person says the USA is already a corporation. USA, Inc. It's listed in Dun & Bradstreet. So are all the cities and towns and agencies. The government doesn't represent the public. What's that about?"

The Transitional Team looked blank.

"Our country is really a big franchise system," T-rump said, "with the federal government at the top, and I'm the new CEO. Everything works through commerce and contracts. The feds borrow money from the banks and hand it out in contracts, and America gets built according to the contracts, which are all New World Order systems and plans." He frowned, thinking. "Do you understand what's going on?"

Members of the Team gave tentative nods. T-rump put the letter down and patted it with a small two-fingered hand. "Let's look at this one again. I'm not going to fire myself before I even start. We have to figure out how to fix stuff without firing me."

He took another letter from the folder. "This says we need to stamp out Satanism," he said. "Satanists are all over America—behind every bush." He surveyed his Team. "Know any?"

The Team was shaking their heads. "We'll have to find some," T-rump said. "Start looking into it. The American people are supposed to have freedom of religion, but Satanism and serving Lucifer runs the show—up and down and at all the highest levels. Do the American people have any idea of this?" Again, heads shook doubtfully.

T-rump placed his hands on his bulky hips. "We need to make a Task Force on the matters in these letters. A different Task Force for each matter. In fact, we need a Task Force Team. We'll create Task Forces to study every single problem and figure out how to make it right." He jumped up and snapped two gnarly little fingers. "And how we'll do this—is with television!"

He began to pace the room. The Transitional Team shuffled out of his way. His big tail took up a lot of space, often jostling rugs and furniture. "Here's what we're gonna do! The American people will be our giant think tank. We'll have a show on TV called Tank You. The American people will give us their ideas—on live TV—and we'll put their ideas into action. Here's the kicker: we'll use contracts and borrowed money, just like we do now. We'll borrow money and pay it to the people as contractors to make America great again! The people themselves will build the country, using their own ideas, and the money will be their incentive, their reward. That's why the show will be called Tank You. Like it?"

The Transitional Team smiled, nodding brightly.

"Now, about the Satanism. The same letter informs that we have pedophilia—again, all over the place. The Satanists are pedophiles and the pedophiles are Satanists. They use magic symbols in logos and advertising; they're in Hollywood and the music business and the whole of it is Satanic. We have got to stop this because the people are losing their children. Not only are the children lost and missing—hundreds of thousands a year —but the rest of the American children are playing this music and buying Satanic T-shirts and sneakers and their minds are going dark. They're also disappearing in pizza places. We need Task Forces on all these things—Satanism, pedophiles, pizza parlors, the music industry, clothing, advertising … In fact, we need a Task Force on every single conspiracy theory the American people inform us about."

T-rump was pacing with determination now, his tail slithering heavily behind him. The Team had plastered themselves against the wall to get out of the way. "So for the conspiracy theories, we'll need another TV show. It's going to be called You Tink. With a question mark at the end. You Tink?—see? Like they say in Queens. The American people will get up on live TV and explain the conspiracies. Put it all out there, in broad daylight. We'll have a Task Force for each conspiracy and report back. On the same show, a later episode. Then, on the Tank You show, the people will give us their ideas about how to fix it." His tail gave a confident slap. "This is how to drain the swamp! Expose and embarrass them all into submission."

He whipped his burliness around. "Now, here's what we'll do for the children. The pedophilia letter says children in Europe have a personal social worker to watch them from birth. The social worker comes to the house and checks on food and homework and the child's bedroom. If it's not right, they put the kid in foster care. The letter says this is how the pedophilia starts if the child hasn't vanished into a pizza place or been picked up by a black government car with tinted windows and flown to an island.

"So from now on, each American child will get a personal dog. It's going to be a tough dog, a guard dog. If people can't protect the children, animals will protect them. I know, because I'm an animal—reptiles are animals. The dogs will have big teeth. And they'll guard the child like nobody's business. If pedophiles want the child they'll have to get past the dog. The dog will be trained and live in the home and obstruct the pedophiles. Each dog will know his child.

"The best thing about this is that dogs can't be bribed with money. The letter said that CPS, the children's protection service, gets federal bonuses to break up families and place children with foster parents who are bad people. Foster care, see, is part of the pedophilia racket. The foster children are being commoditized—hired out for awful activities to evil people with a lot of money. All these state agencies work by contracts and get federal money to ruin people's lives. Ruining lives is profitable, see, and it's all done with these federal contracts. And that's where we come in. We see to it that our agents—dogs, for instance—have no use for money."

"What if the children are allergic to dogs?" a Team member asked timidly.

T-rump's tail snapped again. "Now that is another issue we'll fix. I learned from these letters that vaccines cause bad health problems—autism, learning disorders, allergies—you name it, they cause it. The American children are getting hellish amounts of vaccinations—it's out of control. We've got to stop that. The vaccinations are making a class of unteachable drones. If we stop vaccinating, the children won't be allergic to dogs or peanuts or huge lists of stuff that get longer every year. Plus, they'll be smart again! We'll have a genius class that isn't all

70

Asian. The letter also said we have to take out Big Pharma and the FDA who are pushing drugs that make people sicker, and we should stop all this chemotherapy. We need Task Forces on all these things." He was trotting happily around the room.

"That's a huge amount of work," a Team member said.

T-rump flapped a little hand. "Don't start moaning to me! Look, we have geoengineering to deal with—the fake weather and all the storms that are freezing the American people's asses off. We have GMOs, fake food. We have the fake money, the Federal Reserve, the big banks. But we're going to keep the fake money and banks around for now since the people are so addicted to these bits of paper that they think they can't live without them because they won't be able to pay bills and buy stuff. We need to tackle this step by step—give the people plenty of fake money to pay their bills and buy things to decorate their houses with to make America beautiful again. The people will get all the contracts themselves! Like I've said so many times, it's all going to be beautiful!"

"What about Agenda 21?" another Team member asked.

T-rump shot her his daggery dino-smile. "I know about that. It was in a letter. They call it Agenda 2030 now. Well, it's going to go nowhere. Because with our fake money corporate government contracts and grants we're going to have the American people make the country the way they want it—and this will be broadcast and discussed on my shows. All the plans will be aired on TV and we'll use a bidding process to give out the contracts, and people will have to show their prior work to qualify for the projects, and we'll make sure every American has his or her turn to do something to make America great. It's a done deal! We'll call it The New Done Deal. Kind of like Roosevelt, only ours will be much better."

"What about taxes?" a male Team member asked. "When and how will we do away with income tax?"

T-rump shuffled for another letter and held it up. "We will not abolish income tax! It's a benign and friendly tax, just as I'm a benign and friendly reptilian, intended only for a small number of American people. The rest of America will be shown how to file proper tax returns—educated returns—and the IRS will finally be taught the true rules about who pays income tax. There are taxpayers and tax payers! I happen to know the difference! It's all in the Constitution and the United States Code, which we are going to make shorter and a lot easier to read. Everyone who doesn't qualify as a taxpayer will get their money back each year—this is how it's all going to be beautiful again. Think of what they can buy with that money! A new kitchen, a new car, a vacation!"

"What about Common Core?" someone asked.

"That," announced T-rump, "is going down the toilet. We are not going to teach the children any more new kinds of math. They will learn all the math I learned, the same way I learned it, with an abacus. It was my favorite toy, and it made me my first million. Small hands, small abacus, and you're good to go."

"What about LGBTQ? Transgender?" came the question. "And the Kardashians …?

"One at a time!" said T-rump. "LGBTQ will have its own country. Just like Israel. We'll find the right place, not near Palestinians or anybody else. As for the Kardashians, they're just another bunch of immigrants, and it's the American people's fault if they watch that show so much. Kardashian! It sounds like a cheap carpet.

"Unisex bathrooms will be out in my reign, and we'll have boys and girls again, just like in the old days. The feminized men are caused by plastic chemicals in shampoo, so we'll go back to glass bottles and good old soap and water. People will just have to be more careful. The dangly earlobes and tattoos, well those appear to be the American people's choices. They're walking into these parlors and paying for a reptilian look that frankly is a lot like mine. Now that's flattering, but I don't insist on it."

A Team member raised her hand. "When you say things like my reign, you sound like a dictator."

"Tank you!" T-rump smiled magnanimously. "Always remind me when I throw my weight around. I'm just cutting my teeth in this new job. But I will not be a dictator—I refuse that. The American people can tell me anything they want on the Tank You and You Tink shows. I insist on it. It's all going to be fair and just and beautiful."

"The mainstream media will bash you," a Team member said.

"Bash away!" T-rump yelled back. "The American people own the airwaves! The lying, bashing media will face extinction because the You Tink show will expose their deceptions. The Internet will be bigger and more popular than ever, and we'll have a show on TV that highlights real researchers. We'll call it Dey Tink. That'll end the media!"

"Are we going cashless?" another question was posed.

"No, we're not going cashless! The people constantly fantasize about paper money, so we'll give it to them in bags. We'll have a FRNs for Rebuilding America program. If the fantasy ain't broke, don't fix it. We have to stick with what works."

"What about the trillions of national debt?"

"It is all because of interest!" T-rump thundered. "Interest is usurious! This is how the world has been bought from under the people's own feet! Those who print the money and charge interest have put their names on everything. The people have foolishly borrowed the money to compete with each other in putting their own names on things!" He sighed. "The people have got to stop competing with each other."

"What about the Flat Earth? Hitler! The Holocaust! The Jews! The Black Pope! MK Ultra! The moon landing! Underground bases! JFK! 9/11! The Iraq War! Gun control! The Sandy Hook massacre! Fake news! The Palestinians! Russia! Putin! Armenian genocide! Syria! ISIS! Ebola! Obamacare! The Singularity!" Questions flew at him like bees from a hive. T-rump jammed his stubby fingers in the cavities that were his ears. If there was anything that drove him crazy, it was frantic, cacophonous, jabbering humans.

"Settle down! We'll handle everything! I told you, the revolution will be televised!"

There was a pause. "What about Monsanto?" someone asked meekly.

T-rump lowered his head. His jaws usually hung open as he lacked lips enough to close on his jagged teeth. He sighed, a sound like a heavy wind. The letters fluttered in the air, along with fronds of his carroty hair. "All those companies— Monsanto, General Foods, General Electric—we're going to break them up. Destabilize, devalue, take away their monopolies. They will have to share and return their wealth."

"It sounds like a dictatorship," someone mumbled.

"Well then, we'll ask the American people what they think we should do! That's the whole point of our TV shows. See, it's going to take time. It's not going to happen overnight. I don't like it, you don't like it, but somebody's got to get their hands dirty and it's us, with the American people picking up shovels too. They can't expect this all to be done overnight with a magic wand."

He surveyed the room. The faces of his Team were not hopeful. He raised a scaly finger-stub. "Okay, so let's start with one thing. How about the roads and highways? We'll create federal grants to fix the roads and highways in every state. This is what the American people complain about the most. If that goes well, say, within a couple of weeks, we'll tackle something else. How about it?"

The Team nodded.

"Okay, so let's get a Task Force together. We have a national deficit, so we'll have to borrow the money. Who wants to volunteer for the Roads and Highways project—the first of the T-Rump FRNs of America Tyrannochanges?"

Donald Junior raised a glum hand. "Fine, I'll do it."

"That's the spirit!" T-rump said. "I like to see a willing soul. We must keep up our confidence. After all, look at me. I didn't outlast the extinction of my species for no reason. I was totally confident that I would become a legend—that I would make it. What the American people need the most right now is a good head on their shoulders and good people skills."

He pondered a second and glanced around. "I'm going to let you in on a secret. There never were any dinosaurs. It was just another moneymaking scam dreamed up by some paleontologists and a couple of museums. Some big animal bones, a little plaster of Paris—it all came out of somebody's imagination. But the thing is people believe it. They believe I and my kind walked the earth eons ago and then disappeared and got turned into Middle Eastern oil. How ridiculous!" He rolled his head and eyeballs.

Then he leaned toward them all. "Here's the thing. I am a figment of your imagination! I never existed, not in all of recorded history, but then I somehow came out of nowhere and ran off with the 2016 election! Can you believe it? How is it possible?"

The Transitional Team was not saying a word. People looked fearful, some very pale.

"I'll tell you how it's possible. It's an example of what the collective conscious can do. I manifested from a thought form—it's called transdimensional creative consciousness, something the American people have got to discover for themselves—and I spoke to them in a language they'd been starved of. I studied the Internet and Twitter, learning how the patriots thought and talked. Then I rose in front of them and used their own words. They didn't care that outside the words I was a billionaire, that I had hotels and casinos and jets and boatloads of things they don't have. All they cared about was that they were hearing their dreams described out loud. This is good people skills, I'm telling you."

"But isn't it lying?" someone murmured timidly.

"The whole way of doing things in this lousy dimension is a big fat lie, if you're going to talk like that! What I did was put pictures in their minds—pictures of how they would like things to be. Every candidate does this—they do it in advertising, sales people do it, schoolteachers even do it! Now that I'm the chief CEO reptilian, my job is to animate those pictures. The American people and I will do it together. Did you notice how I sat in meetings always doing this?" He stuck the thumbs and fingers of each of his funny hands together to make a small triangle. "People saw me. It's on YouTube. It's called the Triangle of Manifestation. Time, space and energy. You choose a time and space and you put in the energy, which is you—your heart. This is how you make things happen, and I was doing it."

"Is that Satanic?" the same speaker ventured.

"That's just ancient!" T-rump smashed his tail. "And it works! How else do you think I got here?" He paced again to calm himself down. "So we'll do projects," he continued, "with the reward going to the people themselves instead of politicians and their pals—the same old chosen few. This will get the ball rolling—inspire all kinds of visions and happiness. If the people descend into disappointment and doubt, it's all downhill from there."

"The people have asked for your tax returns," a Team member reminded him.

"I'm going to show my amended tax returns. I'm going to show everyone how to do amended tax returns and get all their tax money back. They're going to love it."

"You have to do all these things, you know. Otherwise they're going to doubt you too."

T-rump twitched his tail with annoyance. "Of course I'm going to. I'm not a birdbrain. I will model my own changes for the American people. I'm going to lose weight, fit into a smaller suit size, change the school lunches. All this will be done on national television right in front of the American people, like I said. We will have projects galore, spread all over the country, with Task Forces for each one. If our projects outnumber us, we'll just have to find more team leaders with decent heads on their shoulders and excellent people skills.

We'll have sub-teams and more sub-teams, and we'll build them and the country right in the American people's living rooms on national TV. And it'll all be incentivized and rewarded with paper money."

He looked around at the doubtful faces. "You know what T-rump means? T-R-U-M-P? To surpass or outdo. I will surpass the system, outdo it, by using its creations on and against itself. We will continue to borrow fictitious money to keep America flowing, but our number one intention will be to use this fake, borrowed, printed, digital, fiat currency to fix it all, do it differently. It's all about intention—what rolls down from the very top of the pyramid. Right now at the top we have a heart of darkness. If this vision of darkness and deprivation is thrown out and swapped with a vision of health and benefit, it can all be beautiful again! The thing is, will the people themselves cooperate and participate, or will they compete and try to surpass or outdo each other? I sincerely hope not."

He rose to his full, bristling, intimidating height. "We will keep the money flowing. Right into the hands of the people. That's what makes them comfortable and happy. They can sing America The Beautiful and finally feel it. Now, who's ready for lunch?"

The Inauguration Speech

Inside/Out

My fellow Americans,

I address you today from the Press Room at the White House in Washington, D.C. after I have assumed power as your lawfully elected King. This will be a lengthy address, as there is much to be said and much work to be done, due to the extraordinary circumstances that include:

- endemic corruption at all levels of the federal government, including the executive, congressional and judicial branches, and most state and municipal governments;
- regulatory bureaucracies at the federal, state and municipal levels that continue to oppress all but a chosen few and undermine the nation's economic vitality;
- intrusions into our lives by what has now been openly recognized as the Deep State, which consists of multiple factions and cabals that through various governmental and non-governmental agencies, mechanisms and structures, exert extra-legal influence and control over our lives;
- a militarism that has a life of its own; and
- a total loss of public trust in all forms of governance;

all of which has served to undermine the sovereignty, reputation, integrity and security of this country, and the welfare of its citizenry.

Because a super majority of the voters of this nation have become aware of this corruption and usurpation of the legal governance process, you the citizens of the United States have decided that drastic action is necessary and have thus voted, through referendums by the required number of states concurrent with the general election, to change the Constitution in fundamental ways – a constitution shredded by past administrations and now in need of serious resuscitation.

Specifically, you have voted to create a monarchy in which I as your King will rule with absolute powers until my work is done and I decide to step down, at which time I have been empowered to leave in place a governance structure of my choosing which, in my judgment, will endure and maintain the positive changes instituted on behalf of the citizens of this nation.

Ironically, we must use extra-constitutional mechanisms to get back to our constitutional roots – a dangerous course if I were untrustworthy. I intend to prove that through my words and most importantly deeds, and by means of mechanisms I am putting in place, that I can provide an unprecedented level of transparency and freedom.

As you know, I have agreed to accept this position based on the promise that a mechanism be put in place to guarantee my safety and prevent my premature removal from office by assassination or other means. You will see standing nearby, four beings – non-human beings – with special mental and physical abilities – who have been "lent" to us you might say by a friendly alien civilization upon my request to help secure my safety and help fulfill our very important mandate and mission.

Around my body, you may see a haze-like aura. This is part of a protective screen that my associates are able to project. These beings provide a unique level of security as well as insight in that they are endowed with special abilities to see into the future, read thoughts, and detect malicious intent and mendacity. Anyone trying to deceive me, harm me or derail my agenda will immediately be detected so they can be exposed and deterred.

I no longer have the need for any additional security and will be abolishing the Secret Service as of today as the first step in dismantling a bloated federal bureaucracy that has done more to enslave us than serve us, and has failed repeatedly to fulfill its mandate to promote justice and protect our freedoms and liberties.

I have also decided to forgo the customary official inauguration and celebration because:

- We cannot afford it
- We cannot be distracted from our mission to rectify the current critical situation
- I want to send a message to all citizens that the promises I made during my campaign will be acted upon in good faith and with immediacy.

I will instead take questions to clarify declarations made herein. Thus I have invited select members of the press, in particular the alternative press, to this event. We also will host a special blog at *IfIWereKing.US* where any citizen can post a question that the Monarchy will answer in plain English and searchable by subject, time and keywords.

I want to begin with this comment.

Power tends to concentrate. Through the ages, concentrated power has invariably been used to suppress the human potential of the many for the benefit of the few who find endless ways of rationalizing why they deserve to be in charge and advantaged relative to the many.

I intend to use my absolute power to do just the opposite: to create heretofore unrealized opportunity for the individual by optimizing the personal freedom of the citizenry so they might optimize their potential – with the following caveats:

- citizens must shed their victim mentality and be willing to take responsibility for their behavior; and
- in the process of exercising their will and freedom, they must not infringe on the personal freedom of another.

As I have said many times before, *Evil Exists. It is interested in Control, and It has a Plan.*

The Human Race has been lied to for millennia by those seeking power and control, especially regarding the existence of other beings in our galaxy and how they have influenced and continue to influence life on this planet. Many who have attained leadership positions have been members of secret societies, occultists, psychopaths and Satanists. Many have been intentionally compromised by pedophilia. In fact, there is a faction of the human race that has become what some refer to as a "Breakaway Civilization," where taxpayer resources have been used and alliances made with representatives of non-human civilizations to create capabilities, culture and governance structures that have resulted in a highly technologically advanced but amoral parallel civilization of human hybrids.

In a word, many humans entrusted with governance have alliances that regard us as property – their property – and not as beings endowed with divine-given, inalienable rights.

We now have the opportunity to come clean, open our hearts and minds, face reality and embrace the Light by following these principles in an effort to optimize our individual freedom and potential:

- Individuals must be responsible and shed their sense of entitlement and what I call victim/dependence mentality. Responsible individuals have intentional integrity and in turn their choices have integrity.
- Decentralization is preferable to centralization. Local self-sufficiency is key to decentralization. Local food sovereignty based on agro-ecological principles is key to local self-sufficiency. In turn, your new government will strive to create a high-tech, connected network of self-regulating and self-sufficient communities that respect and nourish individual rights and culture.
- Humans are tribal; they thrive in nurturing communities that afford meaningful relationships. Globalism has been a form of tribalism for elites who feel they know best and are

entitled to exert their will as they see fit. Thus globalism has primarily served the interests of elite tribes at the expense of others.

- Governance is contractual and should be based on a concept of mutual aid. Localities are expected to make contractual agreements for the services they deem necessary.
- Cooperation is a natural human state, which may be why so much energy has been exerted to keep people at each other's throats. Divide and conquer and problem/reaction/solution have been key components of a legacy strategy for control of the masses by the few. We will get rid of the headwinds against our natural tendency and desire for peace and cooperation so that our citizens can assert their individual power and be responsible for their own successes.
- Complexity has been used to obscure truth, hide corruption, destroy freedom, and undermine our security and sovereignty. Very simply, if a regulatory or legislative act increases complexity, it should never see the light of day. We are now in a position to get rid of those agents, agencies and processes that have added unproductive complexity to our lives, promoted centralization of financial and political power, destroyed small farmers and businesses and in turn local communities, and given unfair advantage to a few through a litany of legislative and regulatory mechanisms.

As King of the United States, with sole and absolute power over its states, territories, and protectorates, I make the following declarations:

Concerning Official Language and Citizenship

1. Any human in this United States of America is subject to my absolute power.
2. American English as commonly practiced is the official language of the 50 states of the United States of America and any future states. All public signage not in English will be removed and replaced within 90 days. Businesses are allowed to use any supplemental language of their choosing in their marketing materials as long as English has prominence.
3. Members of the armed forces or intelligence agencies of a foreign nation must leave the United States within 14 days. Those leaving can appoint a U.S. citizen to handle their affairs and act on their behalf.
4. Residents with foreign passports and visitor, work or student visas or green cards are eligible for citizenship. All non-citizen residents who have not applied for citizenship already, have 30 days to do so. We will expedite the approval process for citizenship to be completed within 150 days after the 30-day application deadline. As part of the approval process, we will require a special interview in which we will be using advanced technologies to detect truthfulness regarding information supplied on applications, in particular regarding past history and future intentions.
5. Existing visas for study, work and visits will be honored for up to 180 days. Once the visas have expired or the 180 days have passed, non-citizens must leave unless their applications for citizenship have been approved. Within 90 days, we will have published new guidelines for non-citizens who wish to begin or continue to visit, study

or work in the United States 180 days from today. Until then, no new applications will be taken.

6. For non-citizen minors under the age of 16, parents will choose whether or not they wish to apply for the minor's citizenship. Persons 16 years of age or older who are capable of doing so will choose for themselves. Those incapable will be considered citizens.

7. All foreign diplomats and their diplomatic staff currently in or planning to come to the United States are required to pass an interview. From now on, we will have the final say as to who is allowed to operate as a diplomat in this nation.

8. Within 30 days, all non-citizens in the country or entering will be fitted with and required to wear an electronic bracelet with specific biological markers at all times. This will be used to track their whereabouts, nor will they be able to transact business or move freely within the country without it. The bracelet will be removed when they finally exit the country.

9. All citizens will be issued a personal national identity card linked to their unique biological markers. This card is capable of receiving but not sending data, and cannot be used to track, determine whereabouts or monitor activities, communications or transactions. If not in the possession of its authorized owner, it will become blank and inoperative after a designated period of time and if reported lost or stolen, or if the owner is convicted of a crime that involves loss of citizenship. This ID card identifies the holder as a citizen who is entitled to all the rights of citizenship under the Monarchy – rights greater than those of any other sovereign nation on the face of the earth. The ID card replaces all other forms of identification issued by any other U.S. governing body

and will act as a passport for travel anywhere in the world. The ID is necessary because sovereignty begins with knowing who are and are not citizens. Again, this card will never be used to track your whereabouts or monitor behavior and has no RFID or other capacity for surveillance. Counterfeit and tamper-proof, it is purely to validate that you are a citizen. It must be carried with you at all times that you are not on your property.

10. By 180 days from today, these new rules and procedures will arm us with the confidence that whoever is in our country is either a citizen or a non-citizen authorized to be here.

Concerning the Rights of Citizens

1. The Seven Articles of the U.S. Constitution primarily dealing with governance structure are hereby revoked and replaced with the following language:

   This government is a monarchy and I as your King am in charge. Whatever I declare shall be immediately so. Congress and the Supreme Court are hereby abolished.

2. The Amendments to the Constitution will be revised as follows:

   The first ten Amendments, known as the Bill of Rights, were intended to protect the rights of the individual to pursue life, liberty and happiness as he or she sees fit - rights that are not the purview of man but are a divine endowment to each human as a foundation for freedom and justice for all citizens. These rights have been mutilated beyond recognition by the government and its corporate and individual accomplices.

The Bill of Rights is hereby altered to expand those rights and make them impervious to any interpretation by law or otherwise that might restrict those rights.

The New Bill of Rights shall consist of only one comprehensive Right known as the Primary Right and shall read as follows:

The Primary Right: All citizens of the United States aged 16 or above have unlimited right to pursue their life as they see fit, as long as it does not interfere with the right of another to do so as well.

First Clarification: Government's sole role is to protect, nurture and facilitate the Primary Right.

Second Clarification: There is no such thing as government-granted privileges for citizens. No government has the right to grant privileges, only to facilitate the Primary Right. Rights cannot be taxed, licensed or assessed a fee, all of which would be penalties for the exercise of a right. Yet charging of fees for governmental services rendered is not prohibited. For example, the exercise of the freedom to go from one place to another with a vehicle on public roadways is currently defined as a privilege and is licensed and taxed. Under the New Bill of Rights, mobility is a right and not a privilege, and is subsumed under the Primary Right. The elimination of any government's ability to treat rights as privileges will, among other things, change the practice of licensing and permitting throughout the nation.

Third Clarification: The welfare of the collective cannot be achieved by sacrificing the rights of any individual citizen. The collective has no rights – only individual human beings can have rights. Collective rights are derived from those individual rights and can never supersede them.

Fourth Clarification: The right to vote is extended to 16-year-olds now considered legal adults.

Fifth Clarification: The rights of minors under 16 years of age and procedures to deal with abusive, negligent or dangerous acts against minors by parents or guardians will be clarified over the coming weeks. However, no person can be regarded as property of the State. The doctrine of *Parens Patriae*, the right of the state to intervene against a parent, is null and void.

Sixth Clarification: Nothing is a crime unless one individual's freedom to pursue their life as they see fit interferes with another individual's freedom to pursue their life as they see fit. Thus one criminal statute will suffice: The Primary Right. All other criminal statutes throughout our country will become superfluous.

Local juries will adjudicate alleged crimes, i.e. violations of the Primary Right; and through those adjudications a body of guidelines will evolve to help elucidate the practical application of the Primary Right. These adjudications will not have the force of precedent as in our former legal structure; they will only provide guidance for future actions by juries.

Seventh Clarification: There is no such thing as "government property." From now on, only individuals or a group of individuals can own property, with the following exception:

- The Monarchy will be allowed to retain up to 1,000,000 acres of federal land for use at its discretion, the specific location of which will be forthcoming. This is in addition to any military installations housed in various states that it determines are necessary for the defense of the nation.
- Each State government will be allowed to set aside up to 100,000 acres for use at its discretion.
- All national forests, parks and monuments will be put under the operational oversight of a board of governors to be elected by the citizens of the States wherein these properties are located and in accordance with guidelines established by the Monarchy to guarantee the proper care of and accessibility to these natural and national treasures.

Eighth Clarification: All citizens have an ultimate right to privacy, whereas government has no right to privacy. For citizens, the right to know about any person or entity that is involved in governance of any kind at any jurisdictional level is infinite. Anyone trying to interfere with this right is committing treason. But the Monarchy has the right to take measures to identify who are in fact citizens and has an obligation to make that information available to everyone.

Ninth Clarification: Corporations are not human and therefore cannot be persons or citizens. Regulations regarding corporations will be revised to reflect this understanding.

Tenth Clarification: It is critical to understand the distinction between creating guidelines that must be followed vs. giving a governing body the right to enforce. Enforcement and thus prosecution lies with the individual (as we will see), not with the State or a governing body. For example, the Monarchy will create universal guidelines for the use of public roads that will be respectful of the Primary Right, but it will leave the prosecution of behaviors that violate the Primary Right under those guidelines to a process not mediated by an agent or agency of the government, except when disputes between States arise. I will provide further clarity on this point shortly.

Eleventh Clarification: Life or any biological entity or

element cannot be patented.

New Bill of Rights

I will now address how the New Bill of Rights, which consists only of the Primary Right, will impact each of our rights under the previous Bill of Rights – rights which have been consistently undermined in the past at all levels of government.

1. First Amendment regarding freedom of religion, speech, press and assembly.
   a. Government will not interfere with the practice of any religion as long as it does not violate the Primary Right. For example, rituals that violate the Primary Right will not be tolerated. By the same token, there will be no subsidies of religion through exemptions of any kind. Any congregation with any real property or financial assets will be treated as a corporation under the law.
   b. There will be no restrictions on freedom of speech, written or spoken, or thought in any form, and no reprisals for any thought expressed as long as it does not violate the Primary Right. A person cannot maintain that their Primary Right is violated by the mere exercise of an individual's right of expression in whatever way they choose to express it if it does not jeopardize the freedom of another individual, including their health or physical wellbeing.
   c. A free press is meaningless unless it has integrity. Since the following networks have endeavored to

distort reality, obscured the truth, colluded with the very institutions they are supposed to be monitoring, and constantly perpetrated material omissions, media corporations listed below will be dissolved 90 days from today by which time all assets must be divested: ABC, NBC, CBS, MSNBC, PBS, CNN, FOX, New York Times, Los Angeles Times, Wall Street Journal, New York Post, Boston Globe, Washington Post, USA Today, Newsday, Daily News, Chicago Tribune, Time, Newsweek, The Huffington Post, Atlantic, Associated Press.

Pertaining to these named media corporations, 90 days from today the following individuals will be denied participation or ownership interest in any news media company for the next 10 years:

- the board of directors or upper management of forenamed media corporations or their holding company or companies (including senior vice-president and above) that have held those positions within the past 10 years;
- their spouses, children, parents, grandparents, uncles, aunts, 1st and 2nd cousins, nephews and nieces;
- previous spouses or partners and their children, parents, grandparents uncles, aunts and 1st and 2nd cousins, nephews or nieces;
- a shareholder of record that has held at least a 1% interest within the last 5 years of any corporation or other entity that has any ownership interest in such media corporation.

Furthermore, an assessment will be made of the remaining mainstream media corporations to determine the extent to which they have been infiltrated by or collaborated with the Intelligence Community or other representatives of Deep State, and foundations, occult or secret societies, or foreign states, thus undermining their mandate as an investigative press with integrity.

    d. Every community will provide a convenient area where citizenry can assemble freely without interfering with the freedoms of others. The area must be big enough to comfortably accommodate citizens and cannot employ any physical barriers or restraints.

2. Second Amendment regarding Militia and the Right to Bear Arms:

    a. Under the Primary Right, the individual has an inalienable right to defend him or herself and friends, family and community against any threat of aggression intended to cause physical harm or restrict the right to live life as they see fit. Deadly force can be used in the presence of a reasonable expectation of bodily harm from an individual or group of any kind.

    b. Police authority is embedded in and derived from this right of the individual to protect him or herself and for individuals to band together for mutual defense and protection. Therefore there should never be a disparity of force – legal, physical or otherwise – between any policing body and the citizenry, to include restrictions of any kind on:

- selection of weaponry

- how, when or where a weapon is displayed or carried
- ammunition for those weapons.

c. The right to own, carry or transport a weapon of any kind, anywhere and in any way (weapon defined as any device that can be used for defense against the aggression of another individual or individuals) is not tied to membership in a Militia, Military or Enforcement Body. It is a fundamental right that is imbedded in the Primary Right.

d. A Voluntary Citizen Militia to be made up of any citizen 16 years or older will be reestablished as the foundation for defense from the threat of or actual invasion by another sovereign nation, but it will never be used to suppress insurrection or as enforcement against citizens because therein lies a pathway to fascism. In a word, the militia will never fulfill a domestic policing function of any kind. Since the citizen militia is an extension of the individual's right to (1) defend itself against aggression and the violation of its rights, and (2) band together with others for the purpose of mutual defense and protection, it can be used for that purpose; and when acting as an agent for a government body, it can only be used against external threats and not against citizenry.

e. The Monarchy will choose the leaders of each State Militia as well as a National Coordinator for all State Militias.

f. The Military Code of Justice is a violation of the Primary Right. When citizens perform military service, i.e. function as part of the citizen militia in defense of the community or the nation, they retain all of the rights of citizens and can only be prosecuted for crimes against the Primary Right, and only by another citizen, and only judged by a jury of peers. In the end, achieving a disciplined and effective fighting force will be dependent upon the quality and trustworthiness of the military leadership that ultimately must be sanctioned by those who have agreed to serve. As in every endeavor, consensus achieves alignment much more effectively than force.

3. Third and Fourth Amendments regarding property and privacy rights and search and seizure:

   a. A citizen's home and property are their castle. No property owner should be restricted from doing as they please with their property for their own use and the use of their family as long as it does not violate the Primary Right. No fees or license or regulations should apply to any structures or improvements built by an individual on their own property for their personal use. This will require a whole new approach to planning and zoning. My recommendation is that regulation of use and creation of building standards pertain only to property being developed for commercial purposes – for example, residences to be sold rather than lived in by the builder, buildings to be occupied by tenants, buildings wherein the public is invited to conduct transactions, public institutions. When the community needs more coordinated control over commercial development, I recommend that the landowner be allowed to do what he pleases in accordance with commercial building codes unless it is opposed by a supermajority of the community.

The Monarchy will establish national building codes to be supplemented by local communities to accommodate distinctive needs. To prevent complexity, no fees will be assessed as part of any permit or inspection process.

b.   As was stated in the Eighth Clarification above, the citizenry has a total and complete right to privacy, and the government has a total and complete obligation to be transparent. Only individuals have the right to secrecy, not governments. Therefore:

i.   Every governmental body will only retain sufficient information to validate citizenship and track transactions between it and an individual citizen. All information and files regarding every citizen is in the public domain and must remain accessible to every citizen. Additional records may need to be retained for citizens convicted of a crime.

ii. No person's home or vehicle, whether owned or rented, can be entered into or searched in any way by any individual, including individuals acting on behalf of a government, without the consent of the owner or lessor, unless there is a demonstrable immediate threat to the life, liberty or wellbeing of another human being.

iii. No person's real property can ever be seized for any reason or under any circumstances except after a person has been convicted of a crime by a jury of his or her peers. Remember, there is only one possible crime: violation of the Primary Right.

c.   Citizens' thoughts are their own. No devices are to be used to monitor, read, interpret or manipulate a citizen's thoughts without freely granted permission, the only exception being the Monarchy's security detail of non-human creatures that have the ability and right to read thoughts and thereby determine intention and reveal dishonesty in an effort to secure my safety and the success of our mission.

d.   All meetings, notations, actions, communications and interactions involving any matters of governance of citizenry at all levels will be videoed, broadcast in real time and archived. There will be no secret meetings, agreements or alliances made by any governing body, elected or appointed, or by me during my reign. (A note to all who wish to meet with me: if you are not comfortable with having our entire interaction videoed and broadcast, don't bother to request an audience.)

e.   All material records and findings of all governing bodies at all levels of governance will be made public. This especially includes all the records and findings of every organization that has been involved or continues to be involved in the military or intelligence. Except in time of war, all will be made public.

f.   War will occur only when the existence of the United States as a sovereign power is threatened by a foreign sovereignty. Our so called "enemies" know much more about us and also what we know about them than our citizenry does. This is a chance to have a truly open global community that respects individual and national sovereignty. We will strive to set the example by sharing with our citizenry and in turn the world what we know and how we know it.

g.   Thanks to advances in surveillance technologies, the opportunity for nations to hide their intentions and affairs has been eliminated. Now we will make that information available to the citizenry who pay for the collection and use of that information – information that is meant to serve the people and can no longer be entrusted to a select group that views secrecy and control of information as their proprietary privilege, and who inherently cannot be trusted to represent the best interests of the citizenry because of personal agendas, oaths of secrecy, undisclosed alliances and conflicts of interest. These technologies can never be used against a citizen unless convicted of a crime by a jury of their peers.

4. Fifth, Sixth, Seventh and Eighth Amendments regarding legal proceedings, conviction, testimony, military vs. civilian law:

   a. There is only one kind of crime: that which interferes with the freedom of an individual to live life as they see fit and who is not intentionally interfering with another individual's freedom to do so.

   b. An individual can only commit a crime against another individual; therefore, only the individual or individuals against whom the crime has been allegedly committed has a claim against the accused.

   c. There is no such thing as a citizen committing a crime against "the State" or a governing body. A governing body cannot prosecute a citizen; it can only prosecute a non-citizen on behalf of its citizenry.

   d. Any citizen accused of a crime by another citizen is entitled to a trial by jury of their peers consisting of no less than 6 and no more than 24 jurors at the defendant's discretion. The trial must be conducted within 7 days of the accusation.

e. By majority vote, the jurors will select a fellow juror to administrate the trial. As one person cannot stand in judgment of another in a trial, there will be no judges.

f. The assumption of innocence until proven guilty is a cornerstone of American justice. Thus, no one should be incarcerated until convicted. For a period of time there will be exceptions to this provision for specific individuals that I will list later in this address. Electronic devices will be used to monitor what the community views as a high-risk suspect prior to trial so their whereabouts and activities are known prior to trial.

g. Since there is only one crime and therefore one criminal statute, individuals will be expected to understand the law and argue on their own behalf. Nevertheless, an individual defendant or prosecutor can request that another individual act on their behalf to argue the case for/against, if they so desire.

h. There is no possibility of double jeopardy.

i. There are three classes of law:

   i. Civil law involving violation of contracts between individuals or companies;

   ii. Criminal law involving an act committed by one individual against another that violates that individual's freedom;

   iii. Tort law involving a claim of injury by one individual against another individual.

j. Only one class of legal action can be brought by one citizen against another citizen for a claimed offense, whereas multiple classes of legal action can be brought against a corporation.

k. All legal actions are to be heard and judged by a jury of peers of the person against whom the action is being brought.

l. A jury has the right to sentence, pass judgment and administer fines commensurate with the severity of the civil, criminal or tort violation committed. The finding of a jury is always final and not subject to appeal. Only penalties can be appealed and an appeal process for penalties will be established. Fines can never exceed a person's ability to pay within a reasonable amount of time – to be determined by the jury. There will no limit on fines that can be assessed against corporations. Fines will go to the community involved in the trial.

m. An action for a specific violation can only be brought in one jurisdiction, not multiple jurisdictions. A jurisdiction might be the nation, state, or region of a state as defined by that state, including cities, counties, towns, and neighborhoods.

n. Nothing should ever be too complex that a jury of citizens cannot understand and action.

o. In turn, there will be no body of prescribed law per se. Only a body of judgments by juries for violations of individual freedom (criminal), contracts (civil), and injury (tort). Case proceedings and judgments are to be maintained in a web-based database for future reference using voice recognition technology to compile a transcript, and video to record all words spoken during the trial and jury deliberations, along with scanning technology to record all documents.

p. Contract and Tort claims must first go through mediation and should only proceed to a jury trial if mediation fails.

q. The Monarchy will have its own court system to:

i. resolve disputes between states;

ii. decide on acts of treason committed against the nation, treason being defined as any act that violates the new constitution severely enough to warrant life imprisonment, death or expatriation; or

iii. resolve contract disputes or tort claims that a jury in a jurisdiction feels is too complicated to deal with.

r. In this latter case, the Monarchy will look unfavorably on both parties that have failed to resolve their issue via mediation and a jury trial. Penalties will therefore be incrementally more severe and potentially levied against both parties.

s. From my perspective, there is an inverse relationship between the health of a society and the number of its laws and complexity of its legal system.

t. There has always been voter fraud. Electronic voting machines, digitizing the vote and allowing voting software to be treated as protected IP has furthered the possibility of massive manipulation. Digital technology has made the secret ballot into an enabler for tampering. The solution is to no longer allow a secret ballot of any kind involving any matter of public governance. This will make voting integrity possible again. Digital voting without fraud will then be possible since everyone will be able to check that their vote was recorded properly and in turn will have the right to challenge any recorded vote they believe to be inaccurate. A public vote will allow everyone to know where everyone else stands on an issue. With an open voting system, the citizenry could have much more direct input on every issue. A true democracy might then be possible in which the *demos* or citizen body decides policy on every issue using web accessible electronic voting technology and not by a representative who might be bought or compromised.

u. To avoid the tyranny of the majority, any initiatives put to a vote will require a supermajority of at least 65% to pass.

v. As was briefly discussed under the Ninth Clarification above, corporations will no longer be considered as having personhood. Thus officers and board members of corporations will no longer be protected against liability and prosecution. Henceforth, all officers and directors will bear criminal and tort liability for intentional acts that cause damage to people, property or GAIA and for which a claim is made by a citizen. This includes the Nuclear and Pharmaceutical Industries, which have enjoyed immunity, through special legislation, from broad categories of liabilities that the citizenry have heretofore been expected to bear.

5. Ninth and Tenth Amendments that deal with residual rights of individuals and states that are not reserved by the Federal Government.

a. The size of the federal government will be drastically reduced, including Cabinet positions and their associated bureaucracies. Those remaining will be downsized. Decentralizing, "decomplexifying," and making states and local communities more responsible for determining their future are key steps to increasing individual freedom.

b. It is the intention of this Monarchy to decentralize power to the greatest extent possible in an effort to maximize individual freedom in accordance with the

Primary Right, which will in turn optimize human potential.

I will now continue with further declarations addressing the previous amendments in the Constitution and other matters of governance.

Concerning Empire and Our Military

1. It was never the intention of our founding fathers to pursue Empire. It is not mine either. We will no longer seek to impose our will on the world.
2. All territories, protectorates or other entities not included in the 50 states will, as of 180 days from now, be free to pursue their own course as determined by a 65% supermajority of citizens 16 years of age or older in an election to be held 170 days from now. This could include voting to remain as they are, becoming a state, or returning to independent sovereignty status. This includes territories that are currently populated – Puerto Rico, Guam, Northern Mariana Islands, the U.S. Virgin Islands, American Samoa – and not occupied – Palmyra Atoll, Baker Island, Howland Island, Jarvis Island, Johnston Atoll, Kingman Reef, and Midway Islands, Navassa Island, Wake Island, Serranilla Bank and Bajo Nuevo Bank. Those with historical roots to the unoccupied territories will be eligible to vote.
3. Hawaii will have the same opportunity as the populated territories to determine by supermajority vote if it wants to remain a state or return to its independent sovereignty status in an election to be held 170 days from now.
4. As leader of our armed forces, I am recalling all military personnel, equipment and contractors from our bases throughout the world, excepting a contingent of nuclear submarines armed with missiles for the maintenance of

credible deterrence for the near term. Space-based weaponry will remain in place for the time being. (Yes, we have had space-based weapons for years. We have lived in a world rife with disinformation, secrecy and deceit for which the citizenry has been expected to suffer and pay.)

5. All military actions, whether covert or overt, will immediately cease, excepting those that support the safe evacuation of our forces. Our 800+ military bases around the world costing us over $150 billion a year to maintain are hereby closed. We will no longer pursue either neoliberal or neoconservative visions of empire. Instead, we will focus on our adequate defense of CONUS (Continental U.S.) from external threats and attacks by assuring a well trained, well-equipped citizen militia and the rebuilding of our infrastructure, economy and culture.

6. Major constituencies within the military, intelligence, university, banking and corporate matrix have used various ideologies as an excuse and rationalization for the fulfillment of imperialistic aspirations that have wreaked havoc, chaos, death, destruction and misery around the world, violated other nations' sovereignty, and served to fundamentally undermine the security, freedom and wellbeing of our citizenry. Our quest for Empire will stop as of today. Our power will come primarily from living ethical lives and setting an example that others with good intentions will emulate so that the United States of America will be viewed as trustworthy again and good folks will want to associate and collaborate with us again. Eschewing empire in turn provides opportunities for de-escalation of global conflict and global de-militarization. Huge resources have been spent to keep the world at war. We will eliminate those internal dynamics and encourage other nations to do the same. For the first time in centuries, we will "give peace a chance"!

7. As of today we are withdrawing from all military treaties. Any alliances will be reevaluated in terms of our new ethic: Live and Let Live.
8. We are withdrawing from our membership in and support for the United Nations and will immediately close the UN headquarters in New York. In too many ways, the UN has acted as a Trojan horse for the creation of a highly centralized, bureaucratic, fascist world government often referred to as the New World Order by the global elite, former presidents and government officials. We will no longer support this objective. There will be many opportunities to foster cooperation among nations. I have determined that structures like the UN, NATO, World Bank and IMF have been put in place by globalists as mechanisms of imperialism and control and not world peace, justice and respect for national and individual sovereignty.
9. All trade treaties are hereby annulled. Trade contracts will be arranged with nations on an individual basis, not on a unilateral basis by region or continent.
10. The manufacture of all nuclear weaponry will be immediately discontinued. We will decommission our land- and sea-based nuclear arsenal over the next two years, except for a core deterrent capability. We expect other nations with nuclear arsenals – Russia, China, North Korea, Israel, Pakistan, India and former NATO member countries – to do the same. After removing the excuse for others not to do so, we will explore ways to increase their incentive to follow in our footsteps.
11. However, the U.S. and other nations also have powerful space- and land-based weapons capabilities heretofore undisclosed to citizens but largely known by the intelligence services of most nations. In many ways, this *directed energy weaponry* makes a nuclear arsenal obsolete – weapons

capable of generating scalar power that can target with precision. Some of these electromagnetic systems have been used to alter weather and mimic natural disasters (earthquakes, tsunamis, cyclones and hurricanes) as well as target, harass and murder individuals. No one has been more deceived than American citizens as to what weaponry we have developed and now deploy.

12. The *Breakaway Civilization* faction, mentioned earlier, has capabilities and intentions that are still unknown. What threat, if any, this group poses is yet to be determined.

13. Transparency will be our antidote to lawlessness and corruption. We intend through our sophisticated intelligence capabilities to make the activities of all nations transparent to all nations, including our own activities. We invite all nations to do the same.

Concerning Money

1. In 30 days, all U.S. paper and coin currency will be worthless, the exceptions being silver and gold coins and notes backed by silver or gold previously issued or authorized by the U.S. Treasury since 1776. If redeemed, they will retain their face value. You will have an additional 30 days to exchange your existing currency for new national currency issued by the Monarchy. The value of the new currency will be that of the current currency. Money in bank accounts will be automatically converted – it is only digits, anyway.

2. Effective immediately, the Federal Reserve will have no right or ability to issue currency or any financial instruments whatsoever.

3. There will be no restrictions on the establishment of local or regional currencies.

4. All U.S. sovereign debt instruments held by Federal Reserve banks will represent no claim and have no force or consequence.

5. The responsibilities of the Federal Reserve (and its network of banks) will be transferred to the Monarchy's Treasury Department within 90 days. Coincident with that change and within 360 days from now, no bank will be allowed to exist with assets exceeding $100 billion. Divestitures of assets exceeding that amount will have to be made within 360 days from now. The Monarchy will fast track the formation of new, local and regional banks to facilitate this transfer of assets. Regarding the 20 largest banks based on assets: Beginning 360 days from now and for 10 years to follow, the board of directors and upper management (including senior vice-presidents and above) that have held their positions in the past or currently hold those positions – including their wives, children, parents, uncles, aunts, 1st and 2nd cousins, grandparents and their spouses, former spouses or partner and their children, parents, uncles, aunts, 1st and 2nd cousins and grandparents – will hold no ownership interest of any kind of any bank or be a shareholder of any corporation or other entity that has any ownership interest in banks.

6. Given that all central banks are basically part of a coordinated, centrally controlled network, we are committed to getting to the bottom of who actually operates and controls this network, which is essentially the most elaborate, pervasive and sophisticated mechanism for the centralization and confiscation of wealth and assets ever conceived. With the complicity of legislators in nations around the world, a privately owned entity, whose ownership has never been fully disclosed, has been granted the authority to manage, manipulate, and control the money supply of every nation.

By tying money creation to bank debt creation, individual and sovereign debt has become a means of control, confiscation and enslavement of the vast majority of the human race.

7. We have created huge risk for our traditional market-based economies as well as incentives for behaviors that destroy real wealth by allowing the cancerous growth of a derivative-based, virtual economic universe – a multi-layered alternative economy that is not tied to real assets and does not respect the commitment of traditional economics to increasing human productivity and physical wealth. And yet these financial instruments that are pure fabrications have a profound effect on the prices of all financial assets and in turn the safety, security and stability of all national economies. Therefore, the trading in derivatives is hereby prohibited and all outstanding derivative-based obligations are hereby made null and void. Markets in these instruments are to be trued up based on current market value. In the future, every financial instrument for hedging or commerce must be backed by or directly tied to a physical asset owned or used in conjunction with the person's or company's regular transaction of business.

8. There will be a mandatory holding period for publicly traded stocks and bonds of at least a year and a day, unless the company holding the paper or the company whose paper is being held declares bankruptcy or becomes insolvent. We need to return to an economy that invests in success and win-win, not in speculation or an economy that can be easily manipulated through leverage and shenanigans that produce a zero-sum game where insiders win at the expense of all other players.

9. All home mortgages not held by an individual or a closely held corporation are declared paid in full. All student debt is

hereby excused. Banks or other institutions holding valid and verifiable claims will be granted an equivalent amount of new Monarchy money (asset swap) for the sole purpose of lending to individuals or closely held companies with net worth of less than $50 million at an interest rate not to exceed 4%.

10. Bank reserve requirements and the reserve requirements of any institution whose primary business is lending will be 30% until further notice.

11. A full accounting of our gold reserves will be made public within the next 30 days. Any gold held in trust for individuals or nations will be returned to them as soon as possible.

12. By some estimates, $50 trillion of wealth has been stolen from the American citizenry since WWII through various forms of fraud. A team of forensic accountants and associates will be deployed to "balance the books" of all former and current federal agencies, in an effort to discover where that money went and who benefited. All efforts will be made to recover whatever wealth in whatever form has been stolen and will be used by the government first to rebuild infrastructure and then to satisfy all personal tax liabilities on a proportionate basis.

13. All "health" or "sin" taxes are revoked. Governments have confiscated lots of money by declaring something as "unhealthy" or "sinful" and then taxing the hell out of it, such as with gambling, cigarettes and alcohol. Government is hereby out of the business of legislating morality by influencing behavior and profiting from it. The only rules and regulations that can be implemented are those that protect, uphold and reinforce the Primary Right.

14. The federal income tax – unconstitutional on its face when passed and never properly voted into law by Congress – is confiscatory and hereby revoked. No state shall have the

right to tax income defined as money paid in exchange for labor and services provided by individuals (to be distinguished from investment income). Keeping in mind the huge reduction in the size of government means a huge reduction in overhead and the need for taxation or levying of fees and tariffs. In turn, government at all levels will be responsible for reengineering how it acquires funds to provide services to its citizenry. Recovered stolen money and assets should provide a surplus for many years to come. Getting rid of the income tax will also go a long way to getting government out of citizens' lives, e.g. there will be no reason for the government to compile financial information on individuals anymore nor will this be allowed. Tariffs/taxes on imported merchandise, along with a fee for services model and a surtax on transactions for the purchase of products immediately transferred electronically to government treasury at the time of the transaction will be considered.

15. There will be a 10% tax on any investment income, defined as any income not derived in exchange for labor and services of individuals. It will be the obligation of the individual or institution paying the income to collect this tax and transfer it to a designated agency of the Monarchy when collected.

16. Double taxation will not be permitted, so Estate Taxes are hereby abolished.

17. All taxes will be evaluated for efficacy and fairness. The cumulative total tax burden levied on an individual should never exceed 10% of the average wage paid to the residents of a tax district.

18. The corporate tax code will be reduced to the following regulation: a 3% tax on gross sales revenue will be paid by

all corporations of every type and will be paid on a weekly basis to the Monarchy's Department of Finance.

19. With these policy changes regarding taxation in force, the tax code will be dramatically simplified.

20. In any taxation or fee scheme, the privacy of the individual will be paramount. The power to tax and assess fees will not be used as a way to "get into a person's life" – i.e. as a control mechanism. Government is in the business of serving the citizenry and of facilitating the Primary Right. It has no other purpose. Government is a service industry.

21. Governance bodies at all levels will supply financial statements with integrity. The money they are managing belongs to the people to whom they are accountable. Financial statements with integrity mean line item granularity of every transaction. The Monarchy's Department of Standards will review all existing accounting standards as defined, for example, by FASB, GAO and the EU's IFRS, and create universal standards for financial statements that will link line item expenditures with GPS data providing place-based transparency of every expenditure.

22. We envision a future in which an individual can determine how their tax money will be used beyond any essential services. Basically, they will have the ability to vote with their dollars and to direct the money to those activities they wish to support.

23. All government information is public information, and all requests for information from the citizenry must be fulfilled as quickly as possible.

24. All non-profit organizations (NGOs) are hereby disbanded due to their violation of their charters by shaping public policy and influencing public behavior everywhere around the globe, often colluding with intelligence, military, governmental regulatory, and Deep State agents and

agencies. Non-profits and foundations have been a primary way for elite groups of wealthy tribes to exert control, shape policy and further political agendas with little accountability or visibility.

25. With Estate Taxes and Income Taxes abolished and overall taxation of individuals and companies dramatically reduced and simplified, e.g. corporate taxes = 3% of revenue, no tax on individual income, 10% tax on any investment income – there will be no need for tax shelters or tax deductions and none will be permitted.

Concerning Health and Welfare

1. A citizen's health records are the property of that individual, not of a physician, a governing agency, an insurance company, or any other entity of any kind. It is totally up to the individual with whom he or she shares their information.
2. When a health emergency requires quarantine to prevent the spread of a life-threatening disease from one person to another, and the spread of that disease is felt to be a violation of the Primary Right, any individual can bring an action against the infected person thought to be capable of infecting others by following the same standards and procedures as for a criminal accusation [see "New Bill of Rights" (4)(g-o)] to be adjudicated by a jury of the infected person's peers of their choosing as to whether a quarantine would be advisable. Whenever possible, quarantined persons should be sequestered in their own residences.
3. The current VA hospital network will become a free clinic paid for by the Monarchy, available to anyone 24 hours a day, every day. Every health facility must provide emergency care services to any individual in need and those services will be reimbursed by the Monarchy.

4. The Centers for Disease Control and Prevention (CDC) and National Institutes of Health (NIH) are hereby disbanded. By aligning with Pharma and other profit-making corporations, these government agencies have consistently worked against the interests of public health. A new agency solely responsible for epidemiology will be formed from the most qualified and ethical practitioners of these and other relevant organizations.
5. All vaccinations are immediately suspended until their efficacy and safety can be fully evaluated. This will require a reexamination of the science of immunity and the relationship between the medical and Pharma industries.
6. The use of all Genetically Modified Organisms (GMOs) in agriculture is banned. The use of GMOs in other industries will be suspended within 90 days until the safety of this technology can be verified. Corporations engaged in the production of these organisms will bear the costs of their elimination from the natural ecosphere.
7. The use of all nanotechnology is banned as of 90 days from today until the safety of this technology can be verified.
8. All geo-engineering, including aerial dispersal of nano-substances in jet fuel or otherwise, is hereby suspended.
9. The Food & Drug Administration (FDA) and Environmental Protection Agency (EPA) have failed to protect the public health and are to be shut down immediately to be replaced by the Monarchy's Department of Public Welfare. Failure to safeguard the public health, which is based on safeguarding the health and health options of individual citizens, will hereafter be considered treason. A new process for evaluating the safety of any new chemical, pesticide, biological agent, pharmaceutical, cosmetic or substance intended for application, consumption, ingestion, inhalation, injection or absorption by humans, plants or animals will be

forthcoming. We will evaluate all current employees of Federal and State Health and Welfare organizations and any past and present employees of the corporations that have been regulated by these agencies to choose suitable candidates to serve in the new Monarchy's Department of Public Welfare, which will also be responsible for setting national standards for all regulatory organizations at all levels of governance.

10. All Nuclear plants will be shut down over the next week. A full disclosure of the disastrous ecological consequences of nuclear technologies since WWII will be forthcoming. It is time to come clean on our disgraceful and disastrous experiment with fission-based technologies.

11. All non-ionizing Electromagnetic Radiation frequencies used for communication or transfer of data will be evaluated for their impact on human health and the biosphere.

12. Federal subsidies for health and welfare, including food stamps, will be discontinued within 180 days. It will be the responsibility of the states and their communities to look after the less fortunate. This cannot be managed fairly, efficiently or economically on a federal level.

Concerning Education and Child Welfare

1. The Department of Education will be immediately dissolved.
2. Common Core is hereby banned.
3. Control of local public schools will immediately revert to a citizen-elected board of parents and teachers.
4. There will be no more federal subsidies for education. This now must be financed and supported locally.
5. Federal proficiency testing will be halted immediately.
6. Mandatory vaccination policy is dangerous and in violation of the Primary Right. No government agency or functionary can override the will of the parent for a minor (defined as

anyone under 16 years of age). The parent(s) vested with the responsibility of caring for and raising the child have the final say on how the child is raised, except in cases of abuse.

7. The criminal charge of child abuse can only be brought by a member of the community in which the abuse has occurred or by a member or primary relative of the child (grandparents, uncle, aunt, 1st cousin, niece, nephew). If a jury finds that abuse has occurred and removing the child for its safety and welfare is deemed necessary, then it will be the responsibility of the community to place the child in a suitable home. If the parent, parents or caregiver for a child are killed or incapacitated in an accident, the community will be responsible for placing the child with relatives willing and able to care for the child as determined by the community; if none qualify, then with another household in the community or a nearby community. The doctrine of *Parens Patriae*, the right of state to intervene against a parent, is null and void.

Concerning Transparency and Sovereignty

1. Effective immediately, all non-disclosure agreements signed by any government employees will be null and void. All government employees will be required to report any rules, procedures, processes, regulations, and such that in their opinion violates the New Bill of Rights to the Monarchy's Bureau of Transparency.

2. Records of previous or existing governmental regulatory entities and any entities or individuals having performed or performing contract work for same will immediately become public, along with all future records. Our aim is 100% transparency of anything involving governance at all levels – community, town, city, county, state, federal.

3. All clearances (secret, top secret, and above) are hereby immediately revoked. Anyone with any type of secret

clearance must declare themselves within 24 hours to the Monarchy's Bureau of Transparency.
4. The U.S. intelligence matrix – with the complicity of the legislative, executive and judicial branches of government, networks of banks and financial institutions, foundations, NGO's and universities, and factions in the military – has operated as the world's largest dealer, market maker, and facilitator of both illicit drugs and human trafficking/sex slavery for decades. The War on Drugs has been used to create an international monopoly of control. Not only have agencies of our government destroyed communities through drugs, often targeting specific communities, but they have also facilitated in the creation of a private prison system and enforcement mechanisms to feed that system so insiders might profit from an entire range of prosecutions and convictions. These activities, along with false flag operations such as 9/11 and covert ops, such as the murder of JFK by what has been described as the Secret Team, along with multiple forms of parasitic fraud and financial manipulation, such as the financial coup of 2008, have been used to divert trillions of dollars into insider coffers, while being the primary source of financing for the Deep State and its manifestations, e.g. the Surveillance State and The Security State. In short, we have been subsidizing our own enslavement for decades as a result of fabricated, manufactured and exaggerated threats.
5. All existing federal agencies or divisions within departments or agencies involved with domestic law enforcement will be closed down, except for the U.S. Marshals Service. Under the initiative Operation Coming Clean, the most competent and trustworthy individuals from affected law enforcement agencies will be chosen to identify, investigate and prosecute crimes we believe have not been disclosed.

6. Regarding *Operation Coming Clean*: In order to get a clearer picture of the criminality that has been epidemic for decades, we are temporarily suspending the Primary Right for the following individuals and groups of individuals and considering them to be guilty until proven innocent. They are being placed under house arrest as I speak and moved to FEMA facilities prepared decades ago under previous administrations for the internment of large numbers of American citizens. We will provide a complete list of those who have been sequestered in the near future.

- All previous living presidents and vice presidents
- Present and former federal senators and congressmen
- Present and former supreme court and federal justices
- Present and former governors of the Federal Reserve System
- Present and former Cabinet members
- Executive leadership of the hundreds of federal regulatory and enforcement agencies
- Members of Council on Foreign Relations, Bilderbergers, and Trilateral Commission within our borders
- Neocons and neoliberals to be named
- Executive officers and directors of the following U.S.-based corporations:
  o top 100 companies that have received the most money in the last 4 years as government contractors
  o 10 largest banks
  o 10 largest insurance companies
  o 10 largest non-banking financial institutions and investment firms
  o 10 largest media companies
  o 10 largest IT companies
  o 10 largest telecommunications companies
  o 10 largest food processing companies
  o 10 largest agricultural production companies

- o 10 largest chemical companies
- o 10 largest NGOs
- o 10 largest foundations
- o 5 largest pharmaceutical companies
- Board members and partners of the 50 largest law firms
- Board and operating leadership of the 20 universities that have received the most government contracts over the last 4 years
- Executive leadership of all 16 or so intelligence agencies of the Intelligence Community and DARPA
- Present and former Joint Chiefs of Staff
- Present and former top leadership of the FBI, Secret Service, DEA, ATF, Homeland Security, and other federal and military law enforcement agencies

7. Those above-mentioned and anyone in addition who has ever served in any capacity in any municipal, state or federal governance structure in this nation as an elected, appointed, or hired official or contractor, have 30 days to declare if they committed, were a party to, facilitated or knew of any acts or omissions to act that in any way intentionally or otherwise interfered with the freedom and welfare of any citizen. These parties will have Amnesty for all crimes declared *and only for those crimes declared*. Why Amnesty? To create the incentive for the people who have been responsible for almost destroying our way of life to come clean. We want *full disclosure* so the citizenry will finally know what is true – what has really been going on behind the scenes. I believe that the truth *will* set us free. Now is the time for all to come clean and drag the corrupt machinations of the covert and overt worlds of power and influence into the open.

   1. However, if you fail to come clean about material and intentional criminality that we subsequently discovered

you were involved in or aware of, you will be tried for treason. We will be using advanced lie detection technology during our investigation - tools that the intelligence and enforcement matrix has been using against the citizenry for years; supplemented by new technologies that have been provided by our alien friends.

2. All who are currently in custody and not mentioned above, including felons who have not committed offenses against another human or their property, will be released from custody as soon as possible and given amnesty. We will be shutting down the private for-profit prison system as soon as possible, as well.

Requiring transparency of the covert worlds of the Deep State, Breakaway Civilization, global Central Banking System, and the Secret Societies that are all intertwined, will do more to remove the headwinds against the optimization of human and natural wealth, health, freedom and justice than anything I can think of. Exposing and dismantling this global Military / Corporate / Intelligence / Financial / University / Foundation / Secret Society Matrix that comprises the Deep State is my highest priority. In the past, anyone attempting to do this was derailed either by co-optation, intimidation, blackmail, character assassination or murder. But with the help of our alien friends, we have a unique opportunity to rid the world of this parasitic scourge starting right here at home.

In conjunction with *Operation Coming Clean*, the suppression of alternative energy technologies that have the potential to create energy independence for all humans on Earth, independent of so-called "fossil fuels" and nuclear fission technologies, will cease. Work will begin on educating the public as to what has been known about alternative technologies for decades.

There is a lot more that I could say about the many changes that will be occurring. I have given you a flavor of where we are headed, and obviously a lot of details need to be worked out during this period of transition. But for now we will take a 15-minute break, after which I will return for questions that I hope will further clarify the whys, hows, whens and wheres of our major revolution in governance and national transition.

God cannot bless America unless we are worthy. In other words, "God will not bless a mess." We need to clean up our act so that we can be worthy.

After Break:

I will take questions from the press for the next hour. Before we begin, I want to ask all of the members of the press from the networks and publications that I have slated for dissolution to get up from their seats and move to the back so that members of alternative media and other conventional media outlets not on the dissolution list can occupy those seats. To the mainstream press, I say this: You have lost your right to ask questions because for some time now you have betrayed your mandate of acting as true journalists with integrity. In fact, you have basically been running a disinformation campaign to the detriment of the people who have been depending on you. Your capitulation has made it possible for the agendas of global elites and covert agendas to flourish at the expense of the citizenry. So you can sit in the back and listen. Maybe you will even find a way to report responsibly and with integrity in the little time you have left. Your time of shaping public perception and manufacturing consent is rapidly coming to a close, and I am happy to see it. You have been a disgrace to your profession.

I will wait to take questions until the musical chairs are over.

First question.

Press 1: How would you like us to address you? Mr. President does not seem appropriate anymore.

King: Well, what would you suggest?

Press 1: I really don't think it is appropriate for me to suggest anything!

King: Why not?

Press 1: Because you are now King and it would be presumptuous of your subjects to suggest to the King how they think he should be addressed.

King: Well, first, I am more your servant than you are my subjects. I don't think of you as my subjects – I think that should be obvious from my remarks. Yes, I have power, but I choose to use that power to serve and to liberate the potential of this country by maximizing the freedom of its citizens. But secondly, why would it be presumptuous if "your King" asks for your opinion. Isn't it disrespectful not to offer your opinion when it has been asked for?

Press 1: How about "Your Highness"?

King: Let's try for something else. What else could you suggest?

Press 1: "Sire"?

King: I like that better. Close to "Sir" but a bit more family oriented. Still respectful but not too stilted. Let's try that for a while and see how it works… Actually, however, I think I would prefer "Our Servant" because governance is about service. So let's go with "Our Servant." Continue with your question.

Press 1: OK, Our Servant. It seems to me that you are setting up the dollar for imminent failure and to no longer be viable as the world's primary reserve currency. Why are you doing this?

King: Why are you saying this?

Press 1: I'm sorry?

King: Look, members of the press. Let me tell you how this is going to work. You can't just say something or ask a question and get away with having no responsibility for your words. So when you ask questions, you may get questions back from me before you get answers, perhaps because I want to understand better what you are really trying to say or discover whose interests you are really serving, but also because I want to force you to *think* and be part of the solution, not just recite what you think is a problem.

And don't be shy in the face of authority. We are all subservient to the Truth. Jump in. I will repeat the question: why do you think that what I am doing is designed to undermine the dollar and destroy its viability as a reserve currency?

Press 1: Well, to start with, you are suspending the citizenship of the most prominent members of our financial institutions, banks, and investment banking houses, including former treasury officials, central bankers, and others I am sure will end up in internment camps. How do you think central bankers of the rest of the world will react, especially if, as you describe, they are part of a closely held and controlled network bent on expanding power and wealth, despite the consequences to every other sovereign nation? How will they retaliate now that you have declared war on them?

King: First of all, it is important to realize that the folks you mentioned and the institutions they represent have been waging war on the world for centuries through manipulation, debt issuance, usury, fraud, corruption, usurpation of national sovereignty, co-optation of governmental mechanisms and functions, and on and on. And this nation has been complicit – in fact, we have been the biggest enabler of those behaviors for decades, happy to use those mechanisms as a hammer and participate in the spoils.

So we are not declaring war on anyone but are finally declaring that there *is* a war going on that was declared on us centuries ago, and it is time we defended ourselves. We are fighting this war on two fronts: domestically and internationally. So let's deal with the domestic front first, and I guess the first question we should ask is, how will folks react here at home?

As I said, we are replacing the existing currency unit for unit with a new currency that the government will be issuing itself – not some privately owned corporation – and whose valuation is the same. We won't need bank debt to put it in circulation. No more derivative markets, a primary mechanism for the leveraged manipulation of currencies around the world. We can put as much money into circulation via cash and digits as is needed to make the economy run smoothly – to match the quantities of goods and services produced so that transactions can occur without friction and money supply-caused inflation can be kept at bay. The value of the new currency will match the value of the old so that transactions can continue seamlessly. With the banking and financial leadership on ice, it will be hard for them to interfere with things.

Incidentally, the new currency will not have any of the Illuminati, Masonic or Satanic symbolism on it that the current currency has – symbols that have been working as a mind control mechanism every time you handle a piece of currency or see an image of it.

This time, the currency will be *ours*, not the product of the Federal Reserve, a private corporation that gets wealthy by getting a cut from every transaction and debt issuance and leaves us with the liabilities. It will be the product of the U.S. Treasury on behalf of the citizenry, not a cabal of unnamed bankers who are against everyone's sovereignty, excepting their own.

There are a number of reasons that the dollar has become the world reserve currency. Probably the most important over the past decades has been that we have not been shy about using force or the threat of force and punishing in every way we can think of whoever tries to challenge our financial hegemony. So now the world gets to choose how and what currency or currencies they will use to transact business. Competition will be based on *merit*, which will force us to become excellent again. Welcome to a multi-polar world. Less death and destruction sponsored by us. That's good.

The second major issue is how the world will come to value the dollar, not just tomorrow but longer term. Hopefully, the answer will be "fairly and as it deserves to be valued." Right now, it's a toss-up because free markets have not really been allowed to exist. Only manipulated markets have existed. So now there is an opportunity for free markets to emerge and have the information they need to function efficiently on a more even playing field that will be reflected in a price yet to be determined.

If a particular country or cabal of banksters decides to use the various techniques at their disposal to crash the dollar on the world markets (as we have done to many others in the past), that would be a deliberate effort to harm this nation, its citizens, businesses, and economy (as we have done to others in the past). It would essentially be an act of war. We will know who they are and what they are doing and will make that knowledge available to the world. Then we can see how other countries react, how world press reacts, how citizens around the world react – and then we can decide how we will react. Considering that we can pick people off with directed energy weapons from space, we have a lot of options if someone wants to mess with us – not to mention the enhanced, unique security and detection capabilities our alien friends provide.

By the same token, we are setting an example and creating an opportunity for nations to shed the chains of central banking monolithic tyranny. A lot of nations have wanted to do that, but we have been one of the key co-conspirators in keeping those chains in place, despite the fact that the parasites we are in bed with are sucking our blood, as well. Not a sustainable plan.

So we invite all nations to join the revolution and throw off their financial chains and do what they have to do to regain control of their own currency and wealth generation while being respectful of everyone else's currency.

One thing I am absolutely confident of is that for the long term, a currency built on transparency, the rule of law, excellence, integrity and fair play will be a currency that can be trusted. Otherwise, no one will be able to trust a currency or an entity that issues that currency. Which is exactly where we are now.

Next question.

Press 2: Sire – I mean Our Servant – could you go into some details about how it is that you have "aliens" by your side? Who are they? Where did they come from? You act somewhat nonchalant about the biggest disclosure in human history – not only of their existence but also of how we seem to have been lied to about their role in human history.

King: I was wondering when someone was going to ask this question. Yes, we have been lied to. Yes, intelligent life beyond us exists – more intelligent, more technologically advanced, and in some cases more ethically and culturally advanced, as well. How could it not be so? Several trillion galaxies in our known universe, each with hundreds of billions of stars and many more planets…

In fact, it is important to understand that what we need to achieve is not only a revolution in governance but also a revolution in consciousness. Humans are going to have to step up to the plate in terms of shedding their victim mentality and being responsible beings, or this whole human experiment on this planet won't work. Evolution in the development of life forms is obviously in play here – life forms evolve and tend towards higher complexity on their own. But it is also true that there has been *intervention* on this planet, major intervention. To a large extent, we are the product of a genetic engineering experiment.

In fact, there is much evidence to indicate that life on planet Earth has been the result of a very large geo-engineering experiment. For example, there is substantial evidence that the moon is an artificial satellite placed precisely to foster the development and sustenance of conditions that make water-based life possible. For example, did you ever contemplate how it is that the rotation of the moon exactly matches the rotation of the Earth so that we never see the "dark side" of the moon? Many unique anomalies indicate that the moon may be a monitoring device geoengineered by advanced civilizations.

We will be disclosing a lot of information about this subject, but not right now. It will take months to get disclosures out, followed by years of discussion to untangle what it means for planet Earth and humanity. For right now, get used to the fact that we are not the only intelligent life in this universe, this solar system or galaxy. How could it be possible that Earth could have so much diversity of life and the rest of the astonishingly vast universe have none? Never mind parallel universes and multiple dimensions and intelligence with the ability to move between dimensions.

The cosmos is much bigger and more complex than what we can even fathom. As here, there are lots of factions out there, some what we would describe as pro-human, some not, similar to our planet where an elite have been operating a zero-sum game since the inception of civilization in a cosmos with infinite possibility. *As above, so below*, and vice versa. I hope that this revelation and many others will shape our thinking and in turn our actions so that we are at last going forward and not backward.

As our planet is very special to us, so is it special to other off-planet civilizations, as well. We need to agree upon ways of being responsible and respectful of what this living organism, our planet GAIA has to teach us, as well as what the more ethically and culturally advanced civilizations can teach us.

Press 3: Our Servant, can you go into more detail about the Deep State and Breakaway Civilization? Who are they? What are they up to? What should be our concern? Why have they not thus far been exposed? And what do your alien friends want in return for the services they are providing?

King: Let me start with your last question first.

As I indicated, some civilizations out there want to see us succeed, and by that I mean grow up, become responsible citizens of this solar system and eventually the galaxy, and realize our special potential as sentient beings with unique intellectual and emotional abilities. But we have a lot of proving to do as to our worthiness and commitment to acting in ways that make us worthy. Therefore, we are fortunate to have attracted a group of beings from a civilization interested in responding to the request for guidance and protection that I and other like-minded citizens made – the request to help us find a way to optimize life on planet Earth through the optimization of freedom.

There was a big push in this direction with the founding of our nation and the Declaration of Independence and Constitution. But our founding fathers who claimed to be for freedom while living in a slave-based economy, who viewed blacks as less than human and women not worthy to vote, who catered to the landowner over the working class, who condoned the genocide of the native people, and who believed in the God-given right to pillage, were deeply flawed from the get go. For almost 250 years now, we have been struggling to get the ship of state pointed in a better direction, and we are not there yet.

We now have a new chance to get it considerably more right. Finally, there is a critical mass of the citizenry who wants to see it happen. Thus we are receiving offers of help because in their judgment we are finally ready to receive that help.

The Deep State is made up of many factions, one of which is the Breakaway faction. Right now, the Breakaway faction is the most centrally controlled and aligned. Basically, it is made up of tribes that put their own power and wellbeing above that of all others, believing that they know what is best for the world and willing to do whatever it takes for their team to win. To their mind, they derive legitimacy from the fact that they view the majority of the citizenry as irresponsible, stupid, and untrustworthy. They are committed to getting things done and consider the political process to be too laborious, troublesome, and corrupt, so they operate extra-legally, having figured out ways to finance their activities through their own brand of criminality – drugs, fraud, theft, human trafficking and slavery, financial shenanigans – because for them the end justifies the means.

Many of the leaders in the covert world (as well as their minions in the overt world) are psychopaths. It is estimated that 5% of the population are psychopaths or sociopaths – folks lacking the ability to act morally or empathetically. Governance and enforcement professions attract a disproportionate amount of psychopaths and petty tyrants. Combine the inability to feel empathy with a sense of entitlement and an elitist ideology backed by a well-endowed network and system that breeds, selects, nurtures, programs, and promotes psychopathy and you end up with the mess we are in. Meanwhile, the citizenry – most of whom do not understand that evil exists – become willing to look the other way for treats, thus creating fertile ground for the development of societal cancers. To the psychopaths and elitists, the citizenry is just getting what they deserve and perhaps even want: someone better qualified to run their lives.

Do you see now why I am making such a huge deal out of the importance of shedding the victim mentality and encouraging personal power based on individuals and communities becoming responsible – making intentional choices designed to optimize freedom that then translate into community power?

None of this mess could have happened if enough of us had taken the time to understand what was really going on and become accountable for creating a different world, looking beyond the façade, the propaganda and the mind control, and making the choice to take a stand by not supporting any of it. A lot of mechanisms were built in at the start of this nation to make government answerable and accountable to the people: referendum, impeachment, recall, citizen militia, the vote. But we abdicated our powers and fell for the bull and treats. Time to come clean, grow up, and face reality in order to create a new reality instead of a zero-sum game – a win-win based on human values of integrity that put humans and GAIA first.

Press 4: Our Servant, I am having a hard time understanding how we are going to maintain law and order at home and not be threatened from abroad if we are bringing our armed forces home while dismantling domestic law enforcement agencies. Seems like we are giving the criminals a clear runway.

King: The real criminals have been running things for a long time. How do drugs get onto our streets and infect our communities if the DEA and intelligence agencies, Justice

Department and various branches of the government don't allow it to happen? How does a government that is supposed to be protecting our rights figure out ways to increasingly shred those rights? How does our currency lose 97% of its value since the founding of the Federal Reserve if criminality is not rampant? How does 9/11 happen and the truth remain suppressed – an event that was obviously an inside job killing 3,000+ of our citizens and destroying the evidence of criminality under investigation on many fronts – if criminals are not in charge? How does President Kennedy's head get blown off in Dealey Plaza – a coup d'état involving a huge number of operatives – if the leadership of the FBI, Secret Service, CIA, military, the Vice President, the Chief Justice, the mayor and police chief of Dallas, and on and on are not involved in the act and/or the cover-up? How does a government run by control files – through intimidation, co-optation, blackmail, threats, and murder – happen unless criminals are in charge? How is it that we can be in a constant state of covert and overt war without declarations of war if criminality has not been sanctioned by the branches of government that have the right and responsibility to prevent this from happening?

So we are much worse off with these criminals running things than not. The Security State and the Central-Banking Warfare models have done an excellent job of increasing our insecurity and destroying our wealth while creating untold death, destruction, and misery here and abroad. As it stands, we basically have legalized and bureaucratized criminality. Those cartels, cabals, matrixes, and networks need to be exposed and eliminated. We are going to do this in five ways:

- Take away their badges and sequester the leadership that has created the mess;
- Create a situation in which the criminals have an incentive to come clean and fess up: by allowing a period for declaration of criminality in order to qualify for amnesty, after which I will go after undisclosed crimes with ferocity while using the information acquired to recover money and assets that have been stolen from the citizenry;
- Decentralize the power to enforce and put it back with the citizenry and their communities, since in a free society governance must be of, for and by the people, including enforcement;
- Create a culture of responsibility and respect instead of entitlement, in which enforcement will become less and less of a factor once folks embrace and live by the Primary Right, an expression of the Golden Rule with a slight variation: do unto others as they would like. Using how you want to be treated by others as the standard by which to treat others is not quite the same as being respectful of how someone else wants to express their freedom and how they want to be treated. The use of force to make people do "the right thing" is a sign of system failure, a wrong mindset to begin with.
- Get the government at all levels but in particular the federal level out of the business of telling folks how they should live their lives. We are not going to micromanage people's lives and use the criminal code to do it. To do so is fascism, the homogenization of behavior, the homogenization of thought. We are for increasing

diversity, the feedstock and end product of robust evolutionary processes so human potential can flourish by maximizing individual freedom in a way that respects another individual's freedoms, as well.

So we need transparency, we need to get rid of the parasites, we need a responsible and empowered citizenry, we need a culture that will foster justice by respecting freedom, we need governance that serves the citizenry, not itself, we need to get back what was stolen.

Press 5: Our Servant, you say that you are going to dismantle large portions of the federal bureaucracy and reengineer the rest, including cabinet positions. Who then will be running things? How will the leadership gap in these areas be filled? How will you manage the transition to this new nation you are envisioning? By edict?

King: Well, things are being run for sure – right into the ground. So the best thing we can do is stop the train before it goes over the cliff. But let's take a look at a few specific examples:

- We don't need a Vice President on the payroll since our alien friends have assured me that there is no need for succession planning during my reign.
- Regarding the Interior Department, we will be transferring all federal land holdings to the States in which those properties reside, except for a small amount of total acres currently under federal control. On the acreage left in the Monarchy's control, I will outsource the oversight and care of those properties to the states in which they are located. We will let the Native Americans and States figure out how to coexist together since those native nations are sovereignties within

States. But we are going to have to reevaluate some of the treaties that were signed recently that have affected claims to water that large numbers of non-native communities depend on. Water is the new gold. We need a *pro rata* sharing of resources, not a specific quantity guarantee to any one group that during times of scarcity could mean no access to water for some, in this case for non-native residents. These treaties resulted from the interplay of several dynamics:

o Making up for past sins;

o Agenda 21/30 whose primary goal was getting folks out of rural communities and into cities to create large swaths of unpopulated reserves in the name of conservation;

o Payback for certain tribes' cooperation with Deep State criminality. Access to sovereign lands within the nation has allowed certain activities to occur on tribal lands that agencies want to keep hidden, as with offshore banking.

Basically, we don't need the Department of Agriculture anymore.

• All agricultural subsidies will be abolished. All they have done is distort what would otherwise be markets subject to supply and demand. National forests will revert to decentralized control. We will not try to dictate agricultural policy centrally. Any rules and regulations involving food will be handled by the Monarchy's Department of Citizen Health and Welfare. Use of genetically modified (GM) technologies in any aspect of food production is henceforth prohibited, as is nanotechnology until its safety can be evaluated.

The Department of Agriculture (USDA) has overseen the debasement of our food, farmland, and water resources, all in service to the consolidation of power over our food resources by a small number of corporations and destruction of ecosystems. GMOs and the chemicals that GMOs are designed to withstand, in particular glyphosate, have been disrupting ecosystems for decades. The USDA has contributed to the promulgation of bad science, the total distortion of free markets, the use of food as a geopolitical weapon, the "terminator seed" and the undermining of the critical seed saving tradition, regulations that destroy diversity, debasement of our forests through years of mismanagement, alliances with industries deleterious to the resources they were supposed to protect… I could go on, but it sounds like criminality to me. In another time, the past and present leadership of this agency and its corporate, financial and political co-conspirators, that have betrayed the public trust in every way imaginable regarding our food, soil, water and forest resources, would be marched to the gallows and guillotines without any due process. Instead, we are giving these criminals the opportunity to come clean and live. But if they don't come clean, perhaps we should consider bringing back public executions?

The Departments of Commerce, Labor, Housing and Urban Development (HUD, a bastion of fraud and abuse), Transportation – Cabinet-level agencies like Energy, Education, Veterans Administration, Homeland Security, EPA, Ambassador to UN, Small Business Association – all little more than pork barrels in need of elimination. Certainly, some functions need to remain, like common defense, adjudicating state conflict, dealing with violations of the Primary Right by governance bodies, adjudicating contract and tort claims not dealt with at a more local, jurisdictional level. But the size of the Monarch's central government will be dramatically smaller than the federal behemoth that has been bred over time.

In fact, while I am at it, let me let the cat out of the bag about a major change.

Washington, D.C. will no longer be the seat of government, nor will the White House be my residence. Most of the government and support buildings will be shuttered. The portion of Washington that has been the seat of government will become a national monument to what went wrong when the seven deadly sins of pride, greed, lust, envy, gluttony, wrath, and sloth displaced integrity and service. The nature of a centralized bureaucracy is that the people in it tend to think everything will work better if they are in control. The federal government created an insulated world, a twilight zone out of touch with reality.

Washington, D.C. was built as a tribute to secret societies, to celebrate the power of hidden control mechanisms that have undermined our freedom and our way of life. The symbolism of Freemasonry is everywhere, from the obelisk to the paintings that form backdrops in the halls of Congress. Washington, D.C. is where representative democracy was conceived as a government for, by, and of the people but was then perverted to morph into a government dedicated to serving what money and influence could buy. The verdict? Life in prison for the entire governmental physical infrastructure for as long as this nation chooses to exist.

As I said, there is a lot to clarify, but the main thrust here should be obvious by now. This nation is entering a new phase of evolution, as is governance around the world. It is time for true human potential to be realized and the chains that have kept that from happening shed. Time to get to work!

See and ask more questions at www.IfIWereKing.US.

Caesar Augustus Trump

Pepe Escobar

The first thing Donald J. Trump could think of the day he woke up not at his gilded palace known in galaxies far, far away as Trump Tower but in an unglamorous, gaudy, deprived bedroom in that House in White remnant of the good ol' plantation days was to unleash a tweet:

"It's good to be the king."

It hardly mattered that it was a blatant rip off of the recurrent punch line in an otherwise unremarkable Mel Brooks flick. After all, Mel was a terrific guy – so why not profit from his irrepressible comic timing?

The White House was no Mar-a-Lago. It walked, talked – and felt – like the set of *Designated Survivor* on Netflix. (*By the way, that fellow Sutherland is not a bad prez either, and his wife, wow, Natasha, she's as hot as Melania.*)

Melania. She did the right haughty thing by remaining at the 66th floor Trump Tower penthouse pad with Barron. Yet she might come out handy in the event of a House renovation. The place better start acquiring a Louis XVI feel to it. Security is fine but obviously better at the Tower. And it doesn't hurt that the deals at the Tower also keep coming. How about that cool $2.195 million for a renovated 1,052 square-foot one-bedroom at the 32nd floor? The buyer must have voted Trump.

It's good to be the king. He's got a super majority vote – well, not really; he actually lost the popular vote, but who's counting? Those Democrat whiners? He's got the unlimited support of the untidy blue-collar masses. He's got a tremendous mandate for change – well, not that tremendous: roughly 25% of the eligible electorate. But what's with those people who never bother to vote anyway? Put up or shut up. He's got full, absolute, undisputed champion of the world authority to do whatever he wants. He dominates Capitol Hill – well, sort of. Gotta do the requisite Paul Ryan dressing down every now and then. The Supreme Court will be in the bag – soon – and he's got Goldman Sachs to run the National Economic Council. What could possibly go wrong? So it's my way or the (dilapidated) highway, the whole lot, by the way, in major need of an upgrade. (*Have you seen the highways in China?*)

Not mingling with the "progressive" barbarians at the gate, devout followers feared for his life. *Now what about all those losers out there? Do they think the CIA will pull a JFK on me? Get real. I've got my own powerhouse security detail adding double trouble to those terrific Secret Service guys. Roll with my arrangement, or die.*

And yet he knew deep down that time was not exactly on his side. *I gotta finish this quick because there's so much to build in this whole wide world. Have you seen Mongolia? There's nothing there – just grass, wild horses, and a few tents. Build, baby, build!*

So much work to do. What's the deal with all those losers in the regime change crowd? The entire establishment in the so-called "progressive" West – neocons, neoliberalcons, Wall Street,

NATO, politicos, all – well, not all of them, because the ones in the know shut up and now want a piece of the action – these losers who wanted to rebuild the Greater Middle East to have it handed over like a peach to the usual suspects, they just can't stop whining like a bunch of sissies because that "We Are The World" One World scheme of theirs has been smashed by an … ignorant, narcissist bully. *What's wrong with narcissist? I'm the best there is. And the best is yet to come.*

Well, I got news for ya, and well, Steve and Kellyanne will relay it anyway. We're overexposed in the world and ultra-underperforming at home. Enough. So no more expensive adventures in that Greater Middle East hellhole, or elsewhere, for that matter. The enemy of my enemy will be my friend – well, even my enemy for that matter. That's what Kissinger told me. He should know.

And that NATO schtick, what a joke. They don't pay! I would scrap them – well, most of them, based on cost-benefit. From now on, what counts is the sum of asymmetrical bilateral interests. The Europeans have to pay up or shut up, and shut up they will, because on top of it they're toast. Ain't got a penny. "Protect" Ukraine? What a dump. Never again.

And the Pentagon guys, oh boy, they need to do their math. The number one security challenge, existential threat, whatever, to the United States is jihadist terrorism, not Russia and China. So we need a coalition. And I'm gonna build a real coalition. Not that sissy Obama "leading from behind" stuff. I'll talk to Putin and Xi. Done deal. And they'll pay most of the bill, anyway. It's in their interest.

China, well, Kissinger told me to go easy. I got it all figured out.

A good jihadi for them is a dead jihadi. So yeah, they are not a "natural" enemy of America. The thing is to reduce our debt with them but without launching a trade war. Navarro will talk some sense to them. I know how to deal with the Chinese: find them a couple of Tang Barbies they would never find in any Hong Kong art gallery secret stash, and you're in business. That Obama TPP thing is dead, anyway – that was NATO on Asia. No wonder no one wanted it, the Japanese, the Malaysians. We gotta strike another deal.

The Russians. Oh, that Miss Universe in Moscow was a beauty. So much real estate property to develop, so little time. General Alexander Lebed was a terrific guy. When he said that my Moscow hotel plans were a litmus test for American capital going to Russia, I had to give him a copy of The Art of the Deal. Of course, Russia is one of the hottest places in the world for investment. If the Four Seasons and the Ritz-Carlton can do it in Moscow, I can do it in Moscow. And Putin did a great job rebuilding Russia, period. We'll get along fine. Smart guy. No-nonsense. This new Iron Curtain stuff is for losers. What we need is an Iron Oven to grill those jihadis.

The Hail Caesar Moment

And then it hit him.
By then, all across the American empire, the outcry in "progressive" circles had reached fever pitch. Stern-sounding punditocracy was proclaiming that tyranny is able to flourish even under a republic façade. Dire warnings that the republic would fall coupled with lofty exhortations about the good of the republic – as if the United States was still a republic and not an oligarchy.

Steve told me about this book by a lofty Brit on Pax Romana. Perhaps Kellyanne could counsel one of her white slaves to give me a pitch. Well, I did find time to go through the start of a chapter and I was stuck by this: the Roman Empire was ruled by absolute power and under the guidance of virtue and wisdom. Why don't they teach these things at Wharton? Now, I could do that. That's me. Build an empire that is prosperous because it is peaceful. Warfare – if any – banished to the faraway frontiers – well, a couple of guys in Somalia. AfPak, who cares?

The Roman Empire stretched from the Atlantic to the Euphrates, from the Sahara to northern Britain. The American Empire is, well, the North Atlantic, a few colonies in that crappy Little Middle East, a few others in Asia, and that's it. Talk about a negative accomplishment.

Donald J. Trump didn't need to read Polybius (in a nightmare?) to realize that Rome was strong because of its politics and military legions able to subdue any other power. *Our politics are crap – I know, I won against all of them combined – and our military badly needs rebuilding. As it stands, we're an ex-Empire.*

And then there was that guy Caesar. The original Caesar. His security detail was certainly not up to scratch. The men who whacked him called themselves "liberators." Ain't no liberator gonna get on my back, with a clean shot no less.

The "liberators" talked about "freedom" like a misguided liberal phony. Donald J. Trump suspected, correctly, that freedom was in fact not just another word for nothing left to lose, but something to be enjoyed by the Roman aristocracy who were supposed to rule and control the whole decision-making process instead of having the whole package monopolized by just one man. Well, why not? What if the man was chosen to rule by destiny (with a little help from Cambridge Analytica) because he was obviously a born ruler?

And that was the moment Donald J. Trump saw the light. He would be the *new* Imperator Caesar Augustus. The power of Augustus derived from his control of an army of more than 60 legions. Well, Trump had the Pentagon – granted, badly in need of revamping (*Gotta bring those costs down, gotta make it stick with the generals that the real enemy are the jihadis*), but still the almighty Pentagon, overlord of the Empire of Bases. And look at the inbuilt bonuses! Imperator Caesar Augustus did not even need to call or regard himself king, much less a mere dictator. He was the *Princeps*, the first Senator, the first citizen, the first servant of the republic.

Trump Princeps. Not bad for a new global resort brand name. Or a yacht. Anyway, technically it was a fact that Rome seamlessly switched from republic to empire, as if it never happened. After all, the empire in theory was still ruled by the Senate, but it was really the emperor – original title: "commander" - who laid down the law.

Caesar Augustus had been an *incremental* kind of guy. All of his powers, one at a time, became increasingly personal. It all happened through due legal process so none of his powers could be taken back unless Augustus said so. Only he could choose at his convenience to give them up. So what if the Greeks – those cynic, stoic, party poopers – called him *autokrator*, autocrat? He was the *de facto* king and he couldn't care less. He had mastered the ultimate Principate.

What better way to deploy the government of a post-everything empire as benign, benevolent, and respectful of law and tradition? Anyway, the United States of America would always remain exceptional on account of its overwhelming military power – well, except for those Russian S-500 missiles and Chinese aircraft carrier killers. But let's not spoil the fun. As in Rome, such exceptional factoids should be milked to oblivion to revert to praise of the New Emperor. After all, his armies were protecting the civilized world. Apart from miserably losing wars in Afghanistan and Iraq, and turning Libya into a wasteland and calling it peace, and leading from behind to turn Syria into a wasteland and calling it – what? Well, those were other regimes than his. The Empire would retreat from the world, anyway. For now.

That subversive preacher from Judea had nailed it: "Render therefore unto Caesar the things which are Caesar's and unto God the things which are God's." So just as Rome under Caesar Augustus infiltrated every single aspect of public life, at home and across the provinces, until it was impossible to imagine a world without a Roman imprint, the New Emperor would impress – actually build – his will over myriad latitudes.

If the Romans had Alexandria, why not a Trumpolitania in the future, replete with requisite monuments to the New Emperor plus public rituals – well, not human sacrifices, ah, the curse of political correctness – to honor his health and vast accomplishments. Imagine a string of communities boasting shrines and major temples dedicated to the cult of America, like Rome linked by rebuilt highways and high-speed rail, in an orgy of first-class infrastructure.

As Rome profited unashamedly from empire, so should America, without ever pretending that the primary motive is the drive to bring order to the world. After all, the Empire of Chaos specializes in promoting chaos and then scrambling to cope with the inevitable blowback. *Ordo ab chao.*

So it was all set. Pence would run the D.C. morass, and Goldman Sachs would run the economy. Donald J. Trump couldn't care less about the free market politicos who had concluded that crony capitalism is fine as long as it is perpetrated by the right cronies. They could feast on the crumbs left from the banquet. What really mattered is that he had identified the new dawn of class struggle remixed. Out with all-out redistribution from the poor and middle class to the wealthy, the stuff of all neoliberal "republics." He would install trickle-down for the poor and middle class, with a little help from plutocratic finance.

And he would be king for life. Enough of this "If I can make it there, I'll make it anywhere." He had already made it. He didn't need to go to D.C. to make it – again. The White House? Revamp it and take it one step beyond Caesar's Palace. From now on, he would be Caesar Augustus Trump.

It's good to be the king. Now get me on that conference call with Putin and Xi.

Navigating the Swamp

Advice for America's New President

Dmitry Orlov

The call to "drain the swamp" in Washington, DC, voiced during the presidential election campaign, resonated with the voters, many of whom have come to hate and despise the Washington establishment. But draining a swamp is a dangerous, uncertain undertaking: unintended consequences can include alligators in the swimming pool and anacondas in the basement, plus there is always the chance that a freak torrential downpour will fill it right up again. Also, draining a swamp takes a great deal of effort to dig, then dredge drainage canals. Wouldn't it be much cheaper and easier to turn the swamp into a toxic waste dump, then bulldoze all the roads leading to it and simply post it off-limits?

That the Washington establishment—a mad tangle of special interests and the federal legislators and bureaucrats in their pay—can be reformed is an idea as optimistic as it is fanciful. Reform is sometimes not entirely impossible, but it is very time-consuming and risky. For example, it took Vladimir Putin well over a decade to bring Russia's lumbering federal bureaucracy to anything resembling good running order, and even today he is still busy arresting and firing officials for corrupt practices. And let's keep in mind that Russia's presidential system gives much more power to its president than the U.S. constitution provides. Even if the Washington establishment can

theoretically be reformed, doing so in under four years—well under four years if there is to be time to demonstrate to the voters that the reforms have been effective—has a chance of success that is practically nil. In attempting reform, the risk and the cost of failure are both extremely high. It is therefore safer to assume at the outset that the Washington establishment is unreformable and to act accordingly—by getting things done while going over its collective head to the largest extent possible.

In essence, the President should act, to the greatest extent possible, as if he had been elected king, not President, and to act as king-like as possible within the ample limits allowed by the Constitution. He should break with the now useless, dysfunctional shibboleths by which Washington operates. He should avoid becoming tainted by Washington, holding all of its officialdom at arm's length. And he should take every opportunity to act directly on behalf of the people, going over the heads of legislators, officials, lobbyists and experts.

Here is a way that the new President can get something done directly on behalf of the people while sapping the Washington establishment of its power: declare an amnesty. The prison population of the U.S. is a huge embarrassment: a larger percentage of the U.S. population is in jail than in any other nation on Earth. The new President can solve this problem single-handedly by pardoning every single nonviolent offender convicted for a victimless crime, such as possession or distribution of cannabis. There are no legal limits to the number of persons the President can pardon. By pardoning all of them in what will amount to an amnesty, the new President will reduce the size of the prison population, de-power all the special interests that enrich themselves through the prison-industrial complex, and create a large block of grateful voters who will gladly vote to reelect the President who freed their loved ones.

Another way the new President can earn a great deal of gratitude directly from the people is by helping them to repudiate onerous debt. For many U.S. citizens, "repudiate" and "onerous" would be new vocabulary words, but once they learn them, they will be sure to like the sound of them. This can be carried out as a phased strategy.

First, the President speaks out against onerous debt, such as that generated by exorbitant charges by doctors and hospitals, by penalties added to educational debt, and by other major causes of personal bankruptcy, explaining that "there is nothing wrong with not paying these debts." This will trigger a tsunami of nonperforming loans.

Next, crack down on debt collection agencies, imposing a zero tolerance policy on them and prosecuting them to the fullest possible extent of the law for even the most minor infractions. This combination will depress the market value of nonperforming loans.

Next, the President can use his considerable personal wealth, along with that of his major supporters, to buy up these nonperforming loans at fire sale prices, extinguishing some of them while accepting partial repayment on others (based on people's ability to pay)—just enough to make this program self-sustaining and marginally profitable. This program—essentially a jubilee—will endear the new President to the large segment of the population, regardless of their political affiliation, who are currently being oppressed by what is essentially debt serfdom.

The new President can take steps to reduce the power of the Washington establishment by championing a new doctrine of regional sovereignty. He can create and empower regional organizations in the form of regional councils that at first function in a strictly advisory capacity whose recommendations to federal departments and agencies would follow as closely as possible but only within that region. Crucially, these bodies must be chosen democratically, in a transparent, region-wide process, so that each candidate is elected regionally. To prevent professionalization of regional politics, term limits are strictly enforced, everyone serving no more than one term.

Creating an intermediate layer of representation between the state and the federal levels would help reduce the power of the two-headed Republican / Democratic Washington hydra accustomed to playing regions against each other in class and culture wars and employing divide-and-rule tactics in order to maintain their grip on political power. If each region is allowed to set its own cultural, social and economic policies, then such divisive tactics become less effective.

Such an effort should likewise be conducive to the President's reelection for a second term, the citizenry in each region being grateful to the President for being granted a greater voice in managing their own affairs. Even if they vehemently disagree with the citizenry of other regions, the President would remain above the fray in that he is the guarantor of the rights of all citizens, allowing each region to decide for itself while preventing it from impinging on the prerogatives of other regions to choose their own path.

The President has great latitude in prioritizing the work of federal officials. Here too he can point them in the direction of regional sovereignty, selectively enforcing or declining to enforce laws and regulations based on the wishes of each regional council. Although the President does not directly control the actions of officials at the state level, there are certain to be numerous possibilities for prompting them to pay greater attention to their regional councils by lavishing attention on those local officials who do so while ignoring those who do not. This again will cause voters in each region and state to favorably view the President as their defender at the national level, for which they will support him and vote for his reelection, regardless of his political affiliation.

Speaking of political affiliation, although the new President is nominally affiliated with the Republican Party, it would be a mistake to view Republicans in Congress as his friends and Democrats as his enemies. Rather, his position should be against both of them and squarely on the side of the American people. Although superficially members of Congress are chosen through a notional democratic process, the system is so heavily gerrymandered that many members of Congress maintain their positions as a sinecure, deeply entrenched and becoming progressively harder to dislodge as lobbyists corrupt them. This is reflected in the abysmal popularity ratings of Congress: rather than being viewed as the voices of the people, these Washington denizens are commonly regarded as servants of corporations and oligarchs. Thus the new President would do well to avoid being tainted by association with any of them. Instead of striving for bipartisanship, he should strive for nonpartisanship by granting or denying access and favor based on questions of strategy and expediency rather than affiliation or party loyalty.

Specifically, the lack of term limits should be considered an overarching concern that colors every single interaction with Congress. Those who have been there for more than two terms should be regarded as political corpses, regardless of their accumulated clout, seniority, or committee chairmanships. The President should communicate only with those who have been in Congress for fewer than three terms and let the entrenched members of Congress fend for themselves, unbriefed, uninvited, not party to any negotiations.

The President should thwart at every turn the typical process of passing by a slim majority huge pieces of legislation with a large number of unrelated amendments designed to please various special interests. Bills passed by a veto-proof margin should be allowed to sail through since there is no other choice, but they should also be deprioritized in terms of implementation, while many of the non-veto-proof bills should be routinely vetoed or allowed to expire unsigned. The President can then choose from among the junior members of the legislature (not the "political corpses") to communicate his wishes to the rest and work on revising these bills to suit. Criticisms of "too much spending" or "too much pork" or "sections drafted by special interests" can always be levied against almost any piece of legislation voted on by Congress. The typical situation of "gridlock" (to be resolved through "bipartisanship") should be countered by the charge of "bipartisan corruption" and "bipartisan collusion with special interests," with a constant drumbeat of claims that members of Congress act only on their own behalf, not on behalf of the people, regardless of their party. The goal should be not to empower this or that faction within Congress but to disempower Congress as a whole.

One ploy that could yield stunning results is to flatly refuse to consider any increases in the federal debt limit at all by announcing that there can be no negotiation on this issue: the debt is already too high, and the only possible topics of discussion are ways of reducing it. Vetoing debt limit increases results in an override, after which the President can then castigate any additional members of Congress who voted to override the veto as being profligate spenders, responsible for pushing the country ever closer to national bankruptcy. If the veto results in a government shutdown, the President can castigate them for failing to do their job, which is to find ways for the nation to live within its budget. Forced to choose between painful cost-cutting decisions and being publicly shamed for bankrupting the country, many legislators would no doubt prefer to propose and vote for significant spending cuts.

Aside from his enemies in Congress, the new President will also have to confront and neutralize enemies entrenched within the foreign policy and defense establishments. Here, it would be helpful to be a stickler for rules by announcing that there will be no foreign troop deployments or military actions and no incursions into foreign territory or waters unless they are explicitly authorized by Congress under the War Powers Act as well as a UN Security Council resolution, or via an official invitation from the internationally recognized government of the country in question. This will largely defang the more troublesome parts of the foreign policy / defense establishment, rendering them defenseless against the charge of "trying to get away with doing things illegally." In addition, the President should announce a new defense doctrine that emphasizes defense rather than offense; under his watch, the United States will never be the first to resort to military force and will only use force in retaliation if attacked.

The defense and foreign policy establishments and the various intelligence agencies offer great possibilities for significant cost cutting. For example, the aircraft carrier fleet costs a lot but is entirely useless against any major, well-equipped military power, now that there are several types of weapons systems that can reliably sink an aircraft carrier. Aircraft carriers are good for terrorizing small, defenseless nations, but is that even a valid mission? Another example is the F-35 fighter, a pure boondoggle entirely noncompetitive with next-generation fighters developed by Russia and China. The new President, acting as commander-in-chief, can consign useless ships to the drydock and useless jets to the hangar, then let those who have championed these boondoggles stand accused of squandering public funds while feathering their own nests.

The new President should also announce that the only defense projects to be green-lighted will be those that deliver on time and within budget, with cost overruns justifying cancellation of the project. This will inject a very necessary dose of discipline into a defense industry used to bloated budgets, blown schedules, and endless cost overruns.

Lastly, the new President should demand that government purchases (especially defense procurements) should be subjected to scrutiny so that any product that cannot be sourced 100% from within the U.S. is regarded as a potential national security risk. With regard to especially sensitive products, such as components and materials used in weapons systems, he should initiate a program of explicit import replacement. This will bring manufacturing jobs back to the U.S. and help offset the effect of cancelling ineffective projects.

One vital area under the President's control is the diplomatic corps that was greatly damaged by largely unprovoked and misguided adventures in Iraq, Afghanistan, Syria, Libya, the Ukraine, and elsewhere. The diplomatic corps should be instructed to stop attempting to bully or micromanage other nations or contribute to their political destabilization, and instead concentrate on forging cultural and economic links. It is a far more effective strategy to bind nations through numerous personal relationships (as, for instance, the U.S. and Canada); such arrangements are exceedingly unlikely to end in war or international opposition. The President must insist on professionalism and high standards for all diplomatic appointments. For example, the ambassadors and their staffs must speak the local languages and have in-depth knowledge of the country's history and culture.

The new President may have to confront a hostile national media. Here, it is helpful that he is an individual of exceptionally high net worth able to privately fund alternative news media organizations whose function will be to punch through the wall of oligarch-controlled mass media. Russia's RT.com, Sputnik.com, russia-insider.com are examples of this strategy. Such an effort could severely curtail the mainstream media's ability to hush up stories, spread misinformation, publish slander and lies and refuse to retract, or hide biases and secret agendas. It might also thwart "fake news" attacks (currently underway) on alternative, non-mainstream news sources. Lastly, it would provide the President with direct, uncompromised access to domestic and foreign audiences.

The new President will have to confront experts of every stripe who claim the authority to recommend and criticize, in spite of a generally pitiful track record of getting it right. This includes:

• Political experts who wrongly predicted the odds of a Hillary Clinton victory

• Economic experts that have been consistently speaking out in favor of the so-called free trade that has destroyed jobs and decimated the middle class

• Climate scientists who not so long ago claimed that a new ice age was nigh, then flip-flopped into global warming mode

• Health experts who pushed low-fat diets triggering an epidemic in cancer, obesity and heart disease, and now demand that children be serially vaccinated as a condition of attending school

All the flip-flopping of so-called "experts" has made citizens mistrust them. The new President should let people know that they are free to make up their own minds, and that he won't let them be pushed around and terrorized by the so-called "experts." Given that many of the "expert community" are ensconced in positions that render them immune to the effects of their own errors, the new President should only accept advice from those who have "skin in the game." For example, insurers don't have the luxury of mismanaging risk; when they do that, they go bankrupt. Contrarily, scientists and other experts can repeatedly get things wrong and then apply for more funding to *perhaps* one day get it right.

There are numerous limits to what the next President will be able to achieve during his term in office. The nation is deeply in debt and its financial house of cards can pancake at any time. A legacy of foreign misadventures has ruined the chances for international cooperation, and the populace itself is deeply divided and suspicious of federal authorities. The phrase "I am from the government, and I am here to help," is enough to make many Americans run in the other direction.

And yet there is one area of federal involvement that the new President simply has to get right; in fact, he can focus on it to the extent that it becomes the hallmark of his administration. This is the area of federal emergency management. When people need help (and they do need help more and more often as disasters multiply—natural and manmade, technological, medical, economic), giving them the help they need is the surest way to assure their abiding gratitude. In addition to providing hands-on management of disaster relief, the President should concentrate on disaster preparedness, namely providing guidance and support to citizens who wish to prepare themselves for coming disasters—creating stockpiles of food, water and medicine, arming themselves and receiving firearms and other weapons training, creating evacuation plans, setting up defendable homesteads to which they can evacuate if where they live becomes uninhabitable, and so on. Such initiatives would run counter to the commonly heard public narrative that attempts to paint a rosy picture. But the people know better; they know that when trouble comes, they will need to be prepared.

In summary, the situation the new President has inherited is, in a word, bad. His success in gaining a second term and securing a positive legacy lies in his ability to make the best of a bad situation in a way that the majority of the people recognize as a worthy achievement. To keep the citizenry on his side, he will have to stay aloof from the doomed Washington establishment filled with court experts and jesters, mainstream media mouthpieces, oligarchs and special interests out for personal gain. It will be difficult, but no means impossible.

What Would Solon Have Done?

Elana Freeland

Journal of First Governor of Cascadia, 2020

For weeks now since the broad infrastructure collapse, I've been busy night and day helping my community resuscitate basic human needs like housing, utilities, food, water, etc. The arguments over the CIA's role in dragging down the latest President have died down, but now it is whether the subsequent "acts of God" were intentional or natural, though I suspect that we no longer know what "natural" means anymore, given the geoengineering and GMO technologies to which we've been subjected for decades.

This afternoon, a "Selection Committee" paid me a visit, two each from Idaho, Washington, Oregon and Alaska. Before their visit, I'd become accustomed to the label of "maverick" for my "radical" ideas about democracy as I understand it, especially my idea of structuring political leadership along the lines of maintaining order on the one hand while leaving citizens free to explore what best encourages individuality and initiative on the other. Not in my wildest dreams would I have guessed that my ideas would at last be valued.

But then, desperation has its own needs.

I invited the eight visitors in. Once they were settled, the co-chairs began by stating that probably like me, they were glad to see a criminal era of power come to an end, despite the ravages of the way the end arrived, and that we now had an opportunity not just to start over again but to begin something entirely new.

Silently, I pondered the words "entirely new," hoping they didn't mean more bogus justifications for "progress" that I'd been hearing my entire life. Surely their interest in me couldn't be that my ideas on democracy were "new."

Briefly, we shared what we knew about the nation's collapse, from what we'd seen before communications had shut down (or been shut down) to the rumors we had to go on. No one was quite sure what coastal cities had been swept out to sea, other than Washington, D.C., of course, and Norfolk, Baltimore, and Philadelphia. The Pentagon had moved underground in granite-based Colorado, along with U.S. Space Command and the Intelligence Community, and the nation was under military law, with FEMA's Continuity of Government (COG) ten regions finally activated, each region on its own to repair infrastructure and maintain the order of the day until no one knew how far into the future. Governors were being appointed until popular elections could be reinstated.

Then came the question that thunderstruck me. Would I be willing to serve as governor of Region 10? While the criminal system had been running business as usual, trustworthy leaders with initiative had been consistently passed over, if not marginalized and discredited. Now that the nation lay in shambles, we were needed.

I was handed a draft of responsibilities expected of a regional governor. I took my time reading through the broad powers one might expect of a sovereign or king, with minor checks and balances coming from citizen review committees and advisers. For the first time since the founding of the nation 250 years ago, ten sovereigns would replace one centralized government. If I accepted, what I decreed would be the order of the day.

I cleared my throat. "Any idea how long it will be before the popular vote is reinstated?"

One of the co-chairs responded. "As long as it takes for the regions to stabilize one by one. As we all know too well, we lost our constitutional way decades ago and have a long way back— or forward, if you look at it that way. If the governor's powers seem virtually unlimited, it's because we need to move quickly and surely. We can't afford the time for endless negotiations and meetings. We have to counter chaos with order as soon as possible."

There was something about how the co-chair phrased that last sentence that made me think of *Ordo Ab Chao,* the motto of 33° Scottish Rite Freemasons. I pondered that for a moment, then asked my second question.

"How does the nation's standing army—our military—view its role in the FEMA regions?"

An uncomfortable silence followed. Finally, one of the Alaskans shrugged. "We don't really know at this point where civilian law ends and military law begins. We're assuming that if the region is stable, we'll have no need for military intervention."

"But we're not sure," the Native American woman from Idaho stressed. "For now, the military is busy dealing with the possibility of foreign threats, now that we're so vulnerable."

Which was its original mandate, I thought but did not say. "So it's the Wild West one more time and a reinstatement of the Posse Comitatus Act?" I semi-jocularly asked, not believing for a moment that *Posse comitatus* would ever be allowed again.

She shrugged. "Hopefully it's not the Wild West my people remember."

I nodded, meeting her eyes. Her meaningful look seemed to be saying that I would do well to take the military and the eventual resurrection of its ground- and space-based technology into serious consideration when the regions were at last up and running again . . .

The non-*Ordo Ab Chao* co-chair pulled us back on track. "We've come to you first because your reputation is that of a leader people trust, one who knows how to yoke leadership to real service and not self-interest. Unfortunately, if you accept, we have no idea how long you will be required to serve as governor and can therefore promise you little in the way of future security. We beg you to remain flexible."

Interesting wording again.

The *Ordo Ab Chao* co-chair removed a sheaf of papers from a folder. "Here are our bylaws and affiliations. None of us are in this for personal gain. Our only desire is for a peaceful transition back to a functional, law-abiding society."

His words didn't relieve my overwhelm. I glanced at the mass of paper now in my hands and said I needed time to think. As the committee departed, I was reminded of the rumors of lawless bands roaming Region 10 and the guns loaded and ready by people's doors. I understood: time and lawlessness wait for no man. I promised to have an answer when they returned in the morning. They in turn promised to bring as much information as they could access regarding the state of the nation and the world.

Once they were gone, I whooped and hollered for a while. An opportunity to implement what I'd studied and thought about for decades! Like the Athenian statesman Solon in the 6th century BCE, I had been chosen as archon.

I glanced at the clock we now had to keep wound. Where was Kate, my trusty sidekick? She'd gone to check on older neighbors and should be home soon. I cleared the dining room table and laid out pads of paper and sharp pencils, knowing that she would say yea to the governorship.

Solon's first act had been to cancel all debts. I decided to do the same. I sat down, picked up a sharp pencil, and began to write:

Decree: All personal debts and those of small locally owned corporations—not transnational corporations—are hereby cancelled. We are making a fresh start.

Big transnational corporations like Microsoft and Boeing had mooched more than enough corporate welfare from taxpayers; henceforth, they would be taxed and held responsible for whatever they owed communities. And if the Bill of Rights was reinstated after decades of abuse,

Decree: Protection of corporations as artificial persons under the 14th Amendment[1] is hereby revoked.

Whatever debts the four states of Region 10 owed the now-collapsed federal government would be cancelled, with such monies going toward rebuilding infrastructure.

Decree: Annual federal income tax is hereby discontinued.

Goodbye and good riddance, Internal Revenue Service.

---

[1]   Josh Clark, "Why do corporations have the same rights as you?" *How Stuff Works*, April 1, 2008.

Decree: Home foreclosures that banks and mortgage companies have been unable to sell for six months or more are hereby donated as tax write-offs to shelter families now homeless.

Now that we would be operating as a region,

Decree: The four states of Region 10 (Alaska, Washington, Idaho, and Oregon) are hereby known as Cascadia.

By the time Kate came in the front door, I was in full stride. She was ecstatic that I'd been chosen governor and hurriedly made tea while I read off my first five edicts, each of which she wholeheartedly approved.

"I like the name Cascadia. God knows we need all the unity we can get at this point." She brought the teapot and cups to the table.

Recalling what the native woman from Idaho had alluded to, I wrote:

Decree: The Posse Comitatus Act is hereby reinstated and the National Guard retained as Cascadia's standing army.

"*Posse comitatus?*" Kate sat down and poured tea. "Most Americans have either forgotten or never heard of that old law. Are you sure you're not just trying to make the military see red?"

I felt strongly about this one. "No, that's not my intention. Federal troops have been making their presence known in states for decades, with or without a governor's invitation, and they may continue to enter FEMA regions. But I want it on the books that 'invitation only' visits are expected." I winked at her. "After all, it's the Wild West and we have to try to hold the old guard to the law, however it goes."

Kate's brow furrowed. She liked the idea of my governorship, but not the possibility that it might be dangerous. Still, she had to know there would be tense moments at the very least.

She sighed. "All right, I hear you, but now let's talk about community."

Kate was right: community life would be the heart of starting over, not decrees. The decrees would provide the framework, but communities would be doing their own individual tweaking, each community autonomous and learning from other communities.

"First is community health, real health—not overpaid doctors and Big Pharma drugs," Kate said. "Instead of shoving health to the backburner and calling it a 'personal choice,' let's put it front and center." She glanced out the window. "Have you noticed how clear the skies are now? No chemical cloud cover."

She was right on both counts. American health had sunk steadily since the geoengineers and agribiz had subjected NATO nations to chemical jet trails, GMO foods and vaccinations. I took up my mighty pencil while we fine-tuned what I wrote.

Decree: Each household will commit to a community garden free of chemical pesticides, fertilizers and GM seed. Public funding will match household outlays.

Decree: All adults are expected to spend a minimum of 12 hours attending seminars on basic human health from a wide variety of disciplines: Chinese medicine, Ayurveda, Western allopathic, vegan, raw foods, yoga, exercise, etc. Effects on health of ionized and non-ionized radiation and vaccinations will be included.

Decree: All GMOs ("terminator" seed and foods) are hereby banned from Cascadia. Devices that test for GMOs will be made available at each food distribution center. Local supermarket management will be required to research genetically modified foods to learn why so many nations have banned them. Supermarkets are to be reorganized as mercados to accommodate local produce kiosks as well as products trucked in for sale.

"We'll need to handpick oversight committees to make sure these decrees have teeth, and those GMO testing devices are going to be expensive," Kate sighed, making a note.

The thoughts were coming fast and furious. "And Kate, make a note that we'll need an anonymous suggestion and complaints box with easy access somewhere downtown, maybe in the park."

"Hopefully, there'll be some praise now and then, too," Kate said, smiling as she wrote.

I looked up at her. "It's a shame, isn't it, how for decades Americans have had few opportunities to impact how their communities are run. They've lost their confidence in coming up with solutions and the ability to think critically and impartially. Thanks to isolating factors like television and the entertainment industry, Internet and iPhone, people can no longer tell the difference between a difference of opinion and an attack. It will take time for them to learn to self-govern again and work out differences without resorting to name-calling and backbiting."

Kate had a sudden thought. "I hope they don't fix the cell towers too soon. People are starting to learn to really talk to each other again."

Cell towers. "Kate, we've got to connect the cell towers to health."

I got up and scanned the science bookshelf, at last finding the book with the figure I was looking for.

Decree: Cell towers will not be closer than 400 meters (1,300 feet) from the nearest home or public building.

Kate jumped up and grabbed Neil Postman's *Amusing Ourselves To Death: Public Discourse in the Age of Show Business* (2005). Turning to his description of the Abraham Lincoln–Stephen A. Douglas debates in the 19th century, she read aloud:

> *The first of seven famous debates between Abraham Lincoln and Stephen A. Douglas took place on August 21, 1858, in Ottawa, Illinois. Their arrangement provided that Douglas would speak first, for one hour; Lincoln would take an hour and a half to reply; Douglas, a half hour to rebut Lincoln's reply. This debate was considerably shorter than those to which the two men were accustomed. In fact, they had tangled several times before, and all of their encounters had been much lengthier and more exhausting. For example, on October 16, 1854, in Peoria, Illinois, Douglas delivered a three-hour address to which Lincoln, by agreement, was to respond. When Lincoln's turn came, he reminded the audience that it was already 5 p.m., that he would probably require as much time as Douglas and that Douglas was still scheduled for a rebuttal. He proposed, therefore, that the audience go home, have dinner, and return refreshed for four more hours of talk. The audience amiably agreed, and matters proceeded as Lincoln had outlined.*

> *What kind of audience was this? Who were these people*

*who could so cheerfully accommodate themselves to seven
hours of oratory?*

Neither of us expected Cascadia to go back in time, but with
proper oversight of electronics, Cascadians might actually begin
to read and think freely again, entertain each other more, turn
to each other, share rides, barter.

"Speaking of getting rides," I ventured, "until we know the
disposition of the Big Oil supply to little Cascadia, I think we
should issue gasoline stipends to each household, depending
upon need and numbers."

"As long as buses and trains and shared rides come first," Kate
stressed.

"Good point," I said, writing it down.

*Decree: Public transportation will be given priority over private
gas and oil consumption. Gasoline stipends per household will
be available, depending upon need and numbers.*

"Another oversight committee," Kate groused, jotting it down.

"Not to mention all the people we need to talk to who
specialize in all these areas and will have their own advice on
how to proceed," I groused in return. At least we had past
successes and errors to study. We weren't entirely starting over,
but it certainly felt like it.

I tilted my chair back and ran my hands through the little hair I
had left. "Oh, brother!"

Kate looked up from her notes and smiled. "Feeling a little
overwhelm?"

I got back up and flipped through the DVDs I'd downloaded

over the years. "Yes, I am, but that's not what I'm agonizing over. I'm really going to need your help on this one. It's another bedrock edict, perhaps THE bedrock edict, but I don't know how to do it or even if I can do it, but I know it has to be done."

I found what I was looking for and popped it into the DVD player. It was President John F. Kennedy's secret societies speech. Secret men's groups had murdered him, and as far as I was concerned, secret men's groups had murdered the nation, too. On the monitor, we watched and listened as the Camelot King told it like it is:

> The very word "secrecy" is repugnant in a free and open society; and we as a people are inherently and historically opposed to secret societies, to secret oaths and to secret proceedings . . . We are opposed around the world by a monolithic and ruthless conspiracy that relies primarily on covert means for expanding its sphere of influence — on infiltration instead of invasion, on subversion instead of elections, on intimidation instead of free choice, on guerrillas by night instead of armies by day. It is a system which has conscripted vast human and material resources into the building of a tightly knit, highly efficient machine that combines military, diplomatic, intelligence, economic, scientific and political operations . . .

When the clip ended, we sat in silence. Kate blew her nose and wiped her eyes; she had never gotten over Kennedy's assassination. "Let's do it," she said with resolve.

I looked at her, thinking how much I loved this intrepid woman.

"Hitler banned the Freemasons," I said as we resumed our places at the table.

"For a while," Kate amended. "Russia banned them for a while,

African nations are still struggling to ban them. It's not easy."

"I don't think I can ban them, given their First Amendment protections, but I may be able to come up with a few ways to limit them so we can at least keep track of their political machinations."

I knew several Freemasons and probably more who kept their membership a secret. A lot of men joined because of the male family tradition, and of course joining helped them get ahead in business and politics.

Kate tapped her pencil. "Most don't necessarily join for the esoteric aspects, do they? After they're in, they fall into the various climbing degree traps. Those who only go through the first three Blue Degrees have little idea of what they're getting into or what their annual tithes are actually supporting."

"But even the vows for the Blue Degrees are blood-curdling, Kate. Take the Entered Apprentice vow: '. . . my throat cut across, my tongue torn out, and with my body buried in the sands of the sea at low-water mark, where the tide ebbs and flows twice in twenty-four hours, should I ever knowingly or willfully violate this, my solemn Obligation of an Entered Apprentice.' Do men actually think those ancient vows are just window dressing?"

Kate shivered. "The public needs to know."

"Especially about the oaths that supersede public office oaths." I was getting upset. "Those damn secret oaths have wrecked our legal system. What makes a Brotherhood 'secret' is its practices—membership lists, initiation rites, degrees, oaths, etc."

"So what will you do? Can you make it illegal for public

servants—judges, lawyers, jurors, district attorneys, police and intelligence agents—to be members of secret societies?"

"Yes, as long as the public knows that it's because of the oaths and vows that supersede those of public offices. I'll make it so that if it is discovered that a public servant is a member of even one secret society, however high or low their degree, they will be guilty of a felony. No misdemeanor for this serious breach of trust. Exploiting the freedom of belief protected by the First Amendment and taking oaths of loyalty that supersede public office oaths is tantamount to treason."

Kate murmured thoughtfully, "But how to enforce it?" Her face brightened. "I know! Each Lodge has a Tyler, right? Well, each Lodge that chooses to continue under your new Hammurabi Code"—she smiled at me—"has to have a government liaison responsible for keeping updated lists of members' names, degrees, and positions in society. Like Native American tribes have government liaisons."

"And secret societies are tribal, aren't they? Excellent." I wrote the next two decrees.

Decree: The early American lyceum system is hereby reactivated to educate citizens as to the essential points of successful governance, including why members of secret societies, as in the division between church and state, must be disallowed from positions of public service—executive, legislative, judiciary, intelligence and law enforcement—if we are to have a reasonable expectation of honest, loyal representative governance.

Decree: Members of secret societies are forbidden to serve as judges, district attorneys, lawyers, jurors, military officers, intelligence agents and police at all levels. Brotherhoods or secret societies include but are not limited to Freemason Lodges and their offspring (Elks, Moose, Eagles, Mormons, etc.), Knights of Malta, Jesuits, Opus Dei, Ordo Templi Orientis (OTO), etc. Citizens who are not public servants and choose to join secret societies are required to post their names, Lodge memberships, degrees and positions in society. Each Lodge will appoint a government liaison to provide updated lists upon request. This is not a religious issue but one of retaining honesty and loyalty in public servants.

When we'd worked out the kinks, Kate looked uneasy. "Will Brotherhoods contest the decree under the First Amendment?"

"I doubt it," I answered. "A dispute would have to be publicly aired, and I don't think they'd want that, though I'd welcome the opportunity of secret societies crawling out from under rocks. That's why they conduct covert character assassinations and murders under the cloak of darkness."

"All right," Kate sighed, writing a few notes and trying to throw off a niggling anxiety about her husband's safety. "I love the idea of reestablishing the lyceum, but what about the rest of education? This is an opportunity to fix what has been declining for decades—namely, a good, solid school system not run from Washington, D.C."

"Time to re-read John Taylor Gatto!" I got up again and thumbed through a pile of photocopied essays on the bookshelf, at last grabbing his **New York City Teacher of the Year Award** speech 'Why Schools Don't Educate' from **January 31, 1990.** "Who better to guide us than Gatto, a 30-year teacher?" I turned to the last paragraph. "'Our greatest problem in getting the kind of grass-roots thinking going that could reform schooling is that we have large vested interests pre-empting all the air time and profiting from schooling just exactly as it is despite rhetoric to the contrary.'" Quietly, I added, "You're right, Kate. Our national collapse has presented us with a golden opportunity to make Gatto's dream come true."

Kate was writing. "Right—no 'large vested interests pre-empting all the air time and profiting from schooling' for a long while. So we need another task force, this time of adults and youths."

I sat down skimming the rest of Gatto's speech. "'Independent study, community service, adventures in experience, large doses of privacy and solitude, a thousand different apprentice-ships'…"

Kate nodded. "We'll provide plenty of opportunities for adventures and apprenticeships while getting communities going again, and they'll feel needed because they *are* needed—"

"—and they'll learn on the job. I never realized how like the old America Gatto's 'guerrilla' Lab School was. Think of how community will rebuild the latchkey-TV family, Kate, and the old American sense of everyone being both teacher and student, like the lyceum days."

Fire was coursing through me for the first time in years. "Without television and cell phones and iPads and social media, we'll turn to each other. And without those deadening factories we called schools—and no WiFi in future schools—knowledge will begin to live again and thrill us with its opportunities to understand our human condition."

Tears welled in Kate's eyes as we stared at each other.

I wrote:

Decree: A task force made up of teachers, parents, and students will evaluate the previous public education system and ideas of educators like John Taylor Gatto to advise on new education systems to open in one year's time.

All of a sudden, I grasped the obvious. "The Pax Americana empire-builders divided us into small states instead of geographic regions to maintain centralized power."

"Now, they're probably planning it from Colorado," Kate added ominously.

I slapped my forehead. The insights were coming hot and heavy. "Of course, they are! Just like they used the pioneers to conquer the Wild West, they're planning to use us to rebuild, then they'll take over again. Size matters . . . Ten regions might just work as a loose federation, like the cantons of tiny Switzerland once worked. But if we return to depending on artificial intelligence, those who run AI will run us again. If satellites are still up and running, we'll have big decisions to make in the not so distant future."

"'Sufficient unto the day is the evil thereof,'" Kate wisely advised as she saw the furrow between my eyebrows deepen. "You'll need to talk with Canada about what they're doing, since we share a border." She made a note.

"Which reminds me: Alaska is part of Region 10, our Cascadia, but shouldn't it have its own region, given how far away it is?"

"Discuss it with the two Alaskans on the Selection Committee, at least until telephone connections are reestablished."

At exactly that moment, the phone rang for the first time in days. We looked at each other and laughed.

"Synchronicity strikes," Kate said as she always did when synchronicity struck.

Already, the landline had become a foreign, devilish technology. I answered tenuously, pushing the speaker button so Kate could hear.

"Hello?"

"Houston, we have contact." It was Jeanette at the post office. "Just letting the two of you know that we have local service again."

We laughed again. "Just in town, Jeanette, our area, or . . ."

"Good question. I haven't tried to call out of town yet. Gotta go, though, lots of joy to spread." She paused. "I think it's joy I'm spreading, but a big part of me has enjoyed the silence." She hung up.

Kate stood up. "I'm with Jeanette, though I'd like to check on people like our adult children."

We knew our son and daughter were inland but not much else. I looked more carefully at Kate's face and saw the worry lines.

"You know how resourceful they are, Kate."

She shrugged in a way that said she was worried.

I stood up and hugged her. "I'm sorry. Here I am, caught up in getting the community back on its feet, and now —"

She hugged me back. "I know. You're a one-track kind of guy. I'm going to try to call them and pull together some leftovers for dinner. But I'm warning you: I'm going to bed at 10 p.m. No all-nighter for me."

Out-of-town phone service was sporadic, but Kate managed a static-plagued call to our daughter in Denver, Region VIII. She vouched for her safety and that of her brother in Santa Fe, Region VI. They were in touch.

Relieved, Kate hung up and turned to the kitchen to heat up leftover pasta while I made a quick salad and said, "Let's take a break and watch *My Dinner With Andre*. We haven't seen it in years, and given what we're doing . . ."

Her eyes sparkled. "Oh, yes! Let's set the decrees aside for a couple of hours."

So we popped the film into the VCR and ate, reliving a conversation from the early 1980s and marveling at how prophetic it had been.

> *Andre: Okay. Yes. We're bored. We're all bored now. But has it ever occurred to you, Wally, that the process that creates this boredom that we see in the world now may very well be a self-perpetuating, unconscious form of brainwashing created by a world totalitarian government based on money, and that all of this is much more dangerous than one thinks? And it's not just a question of individual survival, Wally, but that somebody who's bored is asleep? And somebody who's asleep will not say "no"?*
>
> *. . . See, I think it's quite possible that the 1960s represented the last burst of the human being before he was extinguished and that this is the beginning of the rest of the future now, and that, from now on there'll simply be all these robots walking around, feeling nothing, thinking nothing. And there'll be nobody left almost to remind them that there once was a species called a human being, with*

feelings and thoughts, and that history and memory are right now being erased, and soon nobody will really remember that life existed on the planet.

"My God, Kate," I whispered.

"And no one heard the warning because it was entertainment," she whispered back.

We looked at each other, both stunned by her profound insight. Simultaneously, we uttered, "Lyceum." People must learn about the alpha brainwave technology of television and movies.

After she went to bed, I plowed onward, writing decree after decree about ownership of property and goods, freeing marijuana felons from prison and erasing the felonies from their records, closing prisons-for-profit, a task force to study how the criminality of our courts and police forces had worked (policing for profit, civil asset forfeiture, etc.), decentralizing Cascadia banks, encouraging a barter system alongside money and private non-interest loans, setting up a task force to study jobs and salary gaps for services . . .

I needed to sleep. The Selection Committee was due at 11 a.m. I'd have some time in the morning to do a quick review of the decrees I could share with them if they needed an idea of what I had in mind. While brushing my teeth and looking in the mirror, I went over my new catechism: Build a transparent base. A smaller region would be simpler than sea to shining sea. Expose the fact that secret societies founded the United States and formed secret alliances that eventually destroyed us. Be watchful . . .

Good night.

While the governor of Cascadia slept through the wee hours of the morning, a meeting was already in progress across town in a local church basement not that far from Freemason Lodge No. 1. Communications were local at best for most people but apparently not for this select group of six Brothers sipping coffee and eating a breakfast prepared by Job's Daughters while a satellite-linked computer downloaded data. Present were an Idaho banker, an Oregon police commissioner, a Washington State district attorney, a local businessman, and a state supreme court judge with his techie in tow. Almost all of them were former military officers.

They had already listened to the tape of the conversation between the to-be governor and his wife, thanks to the microphones planted in their home by the two Brothers on the Selection Committee. (It had been their decision to reactivate telephone service so they could begin screening calls.) They were now discussing what else might be among the governor's decrees, given that the conversation had ended when his wife had gone to bed. The worst was, of course, already known: Lodge membership disallowed to Brothers in political positions.

They felt like they were in a crisis mode similar to that of French Brothers in 1789.

As dawn progressed into day, they communicated via satellite with the Motherhouse now in Denver (Region VIII) about what to do when the "ethical" candidate accepted. Hasty plans were set in place just before the two Brothers had to leave for the Selection Committee meeting at 11 a.m. They all would meet later for more discussion and arrangements.

As the meeting broke up, each Brother felt the weight of his oaths. Time was short and whatever was to be done would have to be done fast without the benefit of a well-oiled media spin.

War is hell, each thought in his own way. Politics were definitely war and they would do whatever they had to do to save the considerable territory that American Lodges had gained over the past few centuries.

Biographies

Pepe Escobar

Pepe is an independent geopolitical analyst. He writes Op-Eds for Sputnik, RT, Strategic Culture Foundation, TomDispatch, the South China Morning Post and TeleSUR. He was the roving correspondent for Asia Times/Hong Kong for 15 years, also writing The Roving Eye column. Since January 2017, he's back at Asia Times as Editor-at-Large.

Born in Brazil, Pepe has been a foreign correspondent since 1985, based in London, Paris, Milan, Los Angeles, Washington, Singapore, Bangkok and Hong Kong. Even before 9/11, he specialized in covering the arc of Eurasia, including wars and energy wars and lately the New Silk Roads. He's a frequent guest on RT and CCTV and radio shows from the Americas to East Asia. His columns are regularly republished in websites in the U.S., Brazil, and across the EU. Apart from being contributing editor to a number of books, he's the author of Globalistan (2007); Red Zone Blues (2007); Obama Does Globalistan (2009); Empire of Chaos (2014); and 2030 (2015), all published by Nimble Books. He shuttles regularly between Europe and Asia, from Paris to Bangkok/Hong Kong.

Solari - Catherine Austin Fitts
http://solari.com/about-us/catherine/

Catherine is president of Solari, Inc., publisher of the Solari Report, and managing member of Solari Investment Advisory Services, LLC. Catherine served as managing director and member of the board of directors of the Wall Street investment bank Dillon, Read & Co. Inc., as Assistant Secretary of Housing and Federal Housing Commissioner at the United States Department of Housing and Urban Development in the first Bush Administration, and was the president of Hamilton Securities Group, Inc. Catherine has designed and closed over $25 billion of transactions and investments to-date and has led portfolio and investment strategy for $300 billion of financial assets and liabilities.

Catherine graduated from the University of Pennsylvania (BA), the Wharton School (MBA) and studied Mandarin Chinese at the Chinese University of Hong Kong. She blogs for the Solari Report at solari.com.

Elana Freeland

Elana is a writer, ghostwriter, lecturer, storyteller and teacher who has researched and written on alternative issues all her adult life, including the stories of survivors of MK-ULTRA, ritual abuse and targeting. As one of many Americans still haunted by the unresolved televised murder of President Kennedy in Dallas, she spent 20 years researching and writing the fictional American history series *Sub Rosa America* about occult deep politics behind the assassination and subsequent demise of the United States of America.

Elana is now perhaps best known for writing *Chemtrails, HAARP, and the Full Spectrum Dominance of Planet Earth* (Feral House, 2014) and has recently completed its sequel *Under An Ionized Sky: From Chemtrails to Space Fence Lockdown* (to be released in January 2018) about the resurrected SDI "Star Wars" Space

Fence. In October 2014, the Australian magazine *Nexus* published her article "Directed Energy Weapons for Political Control" and Global Research recently published "Planetary Lockdown, Geoengineering and 'The Deep State.'"

Inside/Out

This entity has asked for anonymity. The editors felt that the essay warranted inclusion regardless.

Dmitry Orlov
http://cluborlov.blogspot.com

Dmitry was born in Leningrad, USSR, into an academic family, and emigrated to the U.S. in the mid-1970s. He holds degrees in Computer Engineering and Linguistics, and has worked in a variety of fields, including high-energy physics, Internet commerce, network security and advertising.

Starting in 2005, Dmitry has published hundreds of articles, two books, and five books of essays. He has given numerous talks and interviews, and delivered keynote addresses at many conferences. His work has been translated into many languages.

A decade ago, Dmitry made a dramatic change in lifestyle, trading dependency and financial security for resilience, self-sufficiency and freedom. He gave up on corporate employment in Boston's high-tech sector, sold the condo and the car, bought a sailboat and set off sailing. This experiment has yielded a wide variety of insights into just how far it is possible to downscale and simplify one's lifestyle while remaining productive, comfortable and civilized, which skills and technologies are needed, and which are superfluous. Having to decide which specific elements of technology are appropriate to this lifestyle, which are not and which are harmful, naturally caused him to focus on the wider problem of making conscious and deliberate technological choices.

Jon Rappoport

www.nomorefakenews.com

The author of three explosive collections, THE MATRIX REVEALED, EXIT FROM THE MATRIX, and POWER OUTSIDE THE MATRIX, Jon was a candidate for a U.S. Congressional seat in the 29th District of California. He maintains a consulting practice for private clients on the expansion of personal creative power. Nominated for a Pulitzer Prize, he has worked as an investigative reporter for 30 years, writing articles on politics, medicine, and health for CBS Healthwatch, LA Weekly, Spin Magazine, Stern, and other newspapers and magazines in the U.S. and Europe. Jon has delivered lectures and seminars on global politics, health, logic and creative power to audiences around the world.

The Saker Community of Blogs

http://thesaker.is

The Saker was born into a military family of "White" Russian refugees in Western Europe where he lived most of his life. After completing two college degrees in the USA, he returned to Europe where he worked as a military analyst until he lost his career due to his vocal opposition to the West-sponsored wars in Chechnya, Croatia, Bosnia and Kosovo. After re-training as a software engineer, he moved to Florida where he now lives with his veterinarian wife and their three children. When he does not blog or help his wife at work, he likes to explore the Florida wilderness on foot, mountain bike and kayak or play acoustic jazz guitar.

The Saker Community of blogs is international and multilingual: 7 blogs (Main, French, Russian, Oceanian, Latin American, Italian, German, Serbian) written in 6 languages (English, Russian, French, Spanish, Italian and Serbian on 4 continents (North and South America, Europe, Asia, Oceania) with 4 YouTube Channels (Main, Oceania, French, Italian). The main blog alone gets well over one million page views per month. *The Saker* Community currently has about 100 volunteers, including professional translators.

Sofia Smallstorm

Website: AboutTheSky.com
Blog: www.SofiaSmallstorm.com
Online store: AvatarProducts.com

A graduate of Brown University, Sofia is an independent researcher who has written and presented extensively on hidden agendas and complex events since her work on 9/11. In the process of researching that topic, she discovered the phenomenon of artificial clouds and geoengineering (chemtrails) and thus came to acknowledge the presence of a synthetic biology agenda embedded in the activities that constitute everyday life. Sofia's "From Chemtrails to Pseudo-Life (Parts 1 and 2)" lectures explain the relationships between chemtrails and synthetic biology and chemtrails and radiation biology.

In 2013, she began researching the Sandy Hook Elementary School massacre, resulting in a presentation entitled "Unraveling Sandy Hook in 2, 3, 4, and 5 Dimensions" in which she describes the nature of DHS [Department of Homeland Security] Integrated Capstone Events, also known as multiple-resource exercises or drills.

Sofia's interviews and podcasts can be found on YouTube. She also has a monthly newsletter available by subscription.

All essays were written independently.
No author had the benefit of seeing other authors' work until
all essays were completed.

The discussion continues - visit www.IfIWereKing.US